HERITAGE OF
THE SOUTH

HERITAGE OF
THE SOUTH

TIM JACOBSON

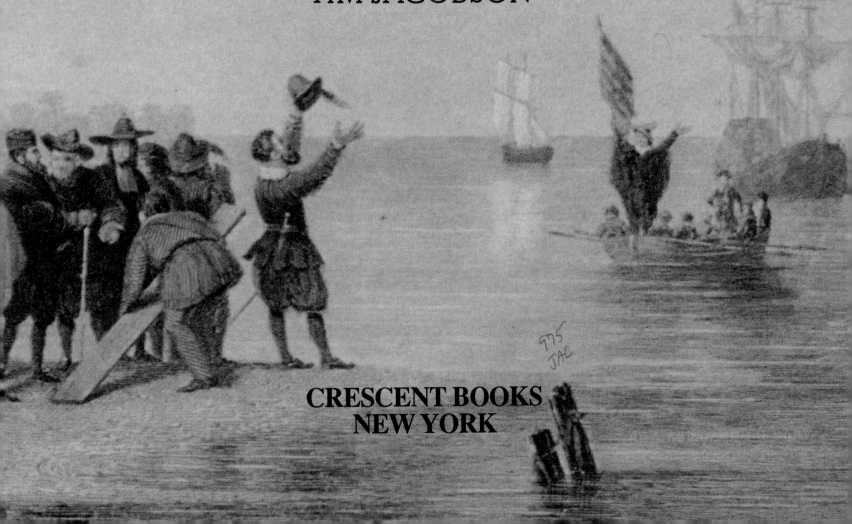

975
JAC

CRESCENT BOOKS
NEW YORK

Editor
Candace Floyd

Photo Research
Leora Kahn
Meredith Greenfield

Commissioning
Andrew Preston
Edward Doling
Trevor Hall

Design
Dick Richardson

Illustrations/Photography
Bettmann/UPI
The National Archives,
    Washington, D.C.
Colour Library Books

GM LT

First page: a pen and ink drawing of men moving cotton bales at a Southern warehouse. By 1820, the production of short-staple cotton, with more than 350,000 bales, surpassed all other crops in the South.

Previous page: a colored engraving of the first English settlers landing at Jamestown, Virginia. These settlers, totaling 120 men, reached the Chesapeake Bay in April 1607 after a grueling four-month voyage across the Atlantic Ocean.

Right: a Currier & Ives colored lithograph depicts the Battle of Chapultapec during the Mexican War, a conflict that many Northerners believed would result in the extension of slavery into new territories.

CLB 2324
© 1992 Colour Library Books Ltd.,
Godalming, Surrey, England.
This 1992 edition published by
Crescent Books, distributed by
Outlet Book Company, Inc.,
a Random House Company,
225 Park Avenue South,
New York, New York 10003.
Printed and bound in Italy
ISBN 0 517 68908 1
87654321

13.95

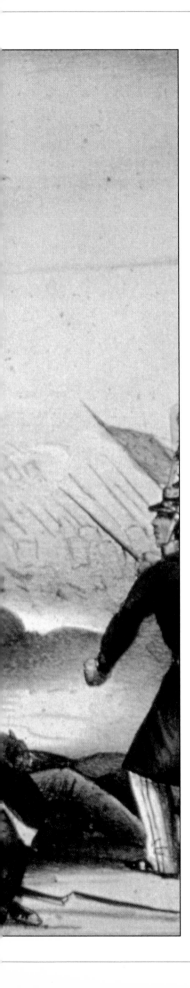

CONTENTS

INTRODUCTION

1
THE COLONIAL SOUTH
page 13

2
THE SOUTH AND A NEW NATION
page 39

3
THE ANTEBELLUM ERA
page 61

4
THE SOUTHERN NATION
page 93

5
THE SURVIVING SOUTH
page 129

6
THE ENDURING SECTION
page 157

7
STILL THE SOUTH?
page 181

THE SOUTH
AS PLACE AND PATTERN
THEMES AND BEGINNINGS

Above: *the Olivier Plantation in Louisiana. As the first rugged settlers prospered in the various Southern colonies, they built up and passed to their descendants huge plantations complete with palatial mansions.*

Right: *Thomas Jefferson, the quintessential Southerner, served as president of the United States from 1801 to 1808. Jefferson was the first of the "Virginia Dynasty," a twenty-five-year period during which Virginia planters served as president. Painting by John Trumbull.*

More than any other part of America, the South stands apart. Some say it's the climate - the thick, oppressive subtropical atmosphere that for eight or nine months every year gives life there a unique quality: men and beasts move slower when it's ninety degrees in the shade. Today however the South has, and has in abundance, air conditioning, interstate highways, franchise fast-food restaurants, and all the other paraphernalia of American consumerist culture. And still it is the South. Thousands of Northerners and foreigners have migrated to it and work happily in its prosperous cities and beguiling countryside, but Southerners they will not become. For this is still a place where you must either have been born, or have "people" who were born there, to feel that it is your native ground.

Natives will tell you this. They are proud to be Americans, but they are also proud to be Virginians, South Carolinians, Tennesseans, and Texans. But they are conscious of the pull of another loyalty too, one that transcends the usual ties of national patriotism or of state and local pride. It is a loyalty to a place where life has always been lived in unique ways, a place where habits are strong and memories long. If those memories could speak, they would tell the stories of a region powerfully shaped by it history and determined to pass some of it along to future generations.

The South's history moves to many themes. Because the South is "Southern" yet "American" at the same time, the theme of sectionalism looms largest. This was especially true during the years before the Civil War, when the American Union was a far more tenuous thing than it would later become. What is important about many events in the history of the South is the way they cast into sharp relief Americans' historically divided loyalties - divided between reverence for nation and reverence for the region, state, or locality closest to them and that they knew and loved the best.

Southerners, in the last analysis, put section and its claims ahead of nation and its claims, and when finally pressed to it they chose to fight a long and bloody war to establish their independence and to protect their liberties and their own ways of living. Southerners in the middle of the nineteenth century were obviously convinced that they were very different. Northerners were too, for they fought just as hard on the other side to coerce the "different" South into becoming more like the rest of the country.

The Southern Confederacy lasted just four years, and the century and a quarter since has seen the South ever more firmly cemented into the structure of American life. What neither civil war nor civil rights nor air conditioning nor the video age could change, however, were Southerners' perceptions, refitted for each new generation, of themselves and their land as things enduringly apart from the rest of America.

The roots of why Southerners should see themselves as different, and why other Americans have often agreed with this assessment, run deep into the soil of this land. Probably what has always to many seemed the most monumental piece of evidence proving the South's distinctiveness was the existence there, until the Civil War, of slavery. Correctly speaking, it was not slavery alone, but the whole pattern of race relations that developed in the South after the death of slavery and lingered into the 1960s. Whatever form it took down through the years, this pattern was a feature of Southern distinctiveness grounded on the existence in the South of large numbers of blacks, who until fairly recently were considered by most white Southerners to be members of a fundamentally alien and inferior race.

Race looms so large in the history of the South because the overwhelming majority of blacks in America were localized in the region. It wasn't that most Northerners were not fully as racist as most

their own without much relation to the facts at all. One such set of images contrasted what was allegedly an agrarian South with an industrial North, and while the facts largely said otherwise - at the time of the Civil War, for instance, the North was as overwhelmingly agricultural as the South - the images nonetheless tell us much about what Southerners were thinking their future might or should be like. Nevertheless, these images had some substance. The first mills were in New England. No matter how fast the South strove to catch up, the North always seemed to have more of everything: railroads, factories, large cities.

Or there were those differing sectional attitudes toward work, which gave rise to images, little altered by the Civil War and its aftermath, of the lazy South and the enterprising North. Here were visions of the hard-bitten New England Yankee, the son of the Puritans who worshipped work for work's sake, and at the end of the spectrum the time-honored figure of the Southern cavalier, that chivalrous guardian of courtly manners and white womanhood whose home was in a generous, easy-going land of broad acres, large plantations, and happy servants.

No one factor predominates, but from the documented facts and the subjective imagery emerges a set of themes close to the core of how Southerners have long lived and regarded their lives. For most of their history Southerners have been a rural people, tied by both necessity and choice to the land and nurtured by a long agrarian heritage. Well into the twentieth century, much of the South existed in a pre-modern era, and even in those places that had been more permeated by change, the shadow of a traditional past stretched long and heavy over the brightest dreams for a different kind of future. Religious orthodoxy or, as it is called today, fundamentalism, has exercised a powerful grip on Southerners from the very beginnings of their culture and has proved highly resistant to the kinds of cultural erosion that elsewhere have accompanied urbanization, industrialization, and the coming of mass society. The details of a particular creed matter less than the impact of a plain and simple faith on the earthly lives of ordinary people.

Southerners, but then it wasn't their problem. Because it was so exclusively a Southern "problem," from early in the game, Southerners came to look on it as something that they and they alone, the ones on the inside, were best equipped to handle. The time would come - from the 1920s through the 1950s, when massive numbers of blacks migrated to the industrial cities of the North and West in search of economic opportunity and an escape from official proscription - when the race problem would cease to be exclusively Southern and would become acutely national. But until then, to think of the South was to think of race, and to think of it in a special way: with white on top and black on bottom with all the formal and informal, legal, and extra-legal devices drafted into service to maintain white supremacy.

As powerful and encompassing as race has been in setting the South apart from other places, race alone does not wholly account for the rich regional identity in which Southerners take such pride. Over the centuries there has developed a whole vocabulary of sectional images and perceptions, sometimes rooted in reality and sometimes taking on a life of

Of equal importance have been Southern beliefs about the proper role of government. In most instances, these beliefs have distilled to a suspicion of centralized power exercised from afar. With deep roots in the debates surrounding the formation of the Union and in the antebellum controversy over slavery, it is a suspicion that has been well watered by later events in Southern history and one that is bolstered by the fact that Southerners have always clung most tenaciously to local attachments and loyalties.

1
THE COLONIAL SOUTH

The permanent settlement of what would become British North America began on the swampy shores of the Chesapeake Bay region in 1607, just four years after the death of England's first Queen Elizabeth and nine before the death of William Shakespeare. It was a time of great ferment, much of it springing from the social and religious turmoil set off by the Protestant Reformation, by the rise of powerful nation states such as England and France, and by the tremendous influx of Spanish gold into the European economy. It was a time that marked a crossroads – a disjuncture – one of those moments when men and the governments and cultures they sustain appear clearly to change tack and to shift their direction toward new goals.

At last, after having known of this continent's existence for more than a hundred years, northern Europeans, and in particular Englishmen, undertook what became one of the greatest cultural transplants in recorded history. What would become the American South was one of its first and most lasting results. Unlike some of her neighbors to the north, such as Massachusetts and Pennsylvania, the land halfway down the eastern seaboard that would become Virginia was not settled according to some grandiose scheme. Its history witnesses no effort to rule men by the power of a single grand, inspiring, or fearful idea. On the contrary, we will understand Virginia and the civilization that developed there and was passed on to the larger South only if we see Virginia as a thoroughly earthly effort to transplant the institutions and the general style of living of old England to the soil of a new wilderness world. If the Pilgrims and the Puritans clung to the rocky shores of Massachusetts Bay in an heroic effort to flee from the Old World's vices, the Virginia colonists hoped to celebrate and fulfill here the Old World's virtues – an Old World with which most of them had no serious religious, ideological, or philosophical complaints. Except in one respect, these were satisfied men.

Above: *a party of colonists arrive by carriage at the Governor's Palace in Williamsburg, the colonial capital of Virginia.*

What drew them across a wild ocean to the edge of a wilder continent was ambition of a largely economic sort, which could find no adequate outlet in the Old World. For decades, the Spanish had been extracting fortunes in gold and silver from their southern American preserves – perhaps Englishmen could do the same.

Sir Francis Drake saw the settlement of the South and the genesis of commerce in the region as a direct attack on Spain's maritime supremacy. During his 1577 voyage around the world, he furthered the English attempts to gain a foothold in the New World by claiming for his country the coast of California, which he called "New Albion," and, not incidentally, by plundering Spanish ships and settlements he encountered. In March 1584, Sir Walter Raleigh obtained a charter from Queen Elizabeth to establish an English settlement in Virginia and explore the region. Members of Raleigh's first band of settlers returned to England from their inhospitable home on Roanoke Island, but Raleigh remained determined to establish an outpost, and in 1587 he again sent 150 settlers to Virginia. Although their original destination was the Chesapeake Bay, these settlers landed first at Roanoke Island and decided to remain there. As the settlers struggled to carve out a niche of civilization, Spain cast its acquisitive eyes toward England, and the English government directed its efforts toward defeating the invincible Armada. When matters in Europe settled down, Raleigh dispatched another expedition carrying supplies and new settlers to the Roanoke colony. What these settlers found when they arrived in 1590 was not a thriving community. All the original settlers had vanished, and the only clue to their demise was the word "Croatan," the name of a tribe of Indians in the area, carved in the bark of a tree.

Despite the mysterious and frightening end of the 1587 lost colony, Englishmen continued to devise new methods of financing settlements in the New World. Joint-stock companies, such as the London Company and the Plymouth Company, were formed with an eye toward maximum profits and minimum risks. To that workaday end, the London Company secured from King James I a royal charter to found a colony in the southern part of "Virginia," as the entire region claimed by England was called. Something of a prototype for the modern corporation, the London Company rested on the principle of limited liability as the means of reducing individual risk while making possible the financing of hazardous overseas ventures. Not quite sure of what they would find, the company sold shares and set about recruiting settlers; the company paid the settler's passage and the latter agreed to work seven years for the company, and only then for himself.

In 1606, 120 men set sail toward Virginia in three ships under the Command of Captain Christopher Newport. Their instructions were to establish a fortified post from which they were to trade with the natives and search for a passage to the Pacific Ocean. The ships reached the Chesapeake Bay in April 1607, after a four-month voyage that claimed the lives of sixteen of the party. The group sailed thirty miles up the James River and selected as their site a densely wooded area bordering a mosquito-ridden swamp.

Indigo Plant.

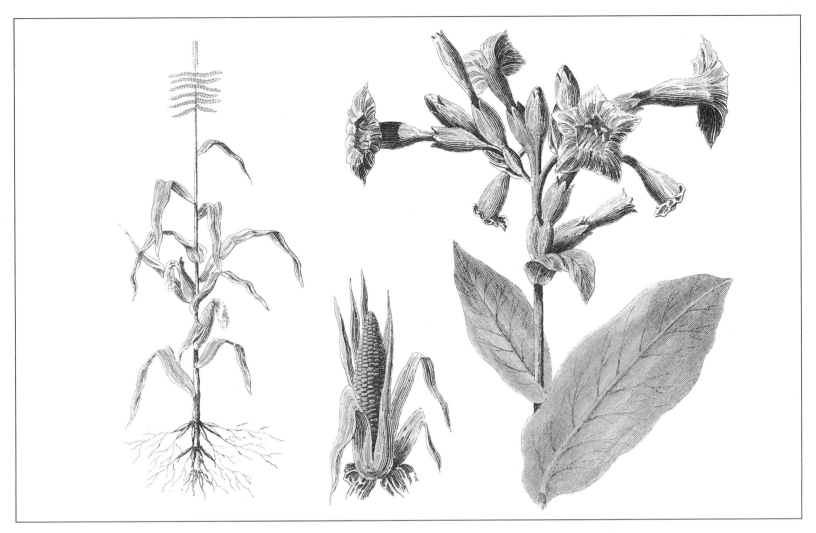

Above: *an early nineteenth-century print of corn (left and middle) and tobacco (right). Tobacco was king in Virginia, North Carolina, and Maryland. Many tobacco planters in Maryland and northern Virginia shipped their produce directly to England from their own private wharves.*

Left: *Ribaut's Fort, South Carolina, a Huguenot settlement founded in the seventeenth century. South Carolina was initally governed by eight proprietors who promoted settlement in the region by promising freedom from customs duties on produce shipped back to England.*

Left: *British merchant ships prepare to anchor off Jamestown, Virginia in 1607. After arriving in April of that year, the settlers fell victim to an epidemic of malaria that killed all but thirty-eight of the original 120 men.*

Below far left: *early colonists at work on the buildings in the Jamestown colony. These colonists had three tasks set out for them: building a fort, planting crops, and exploring the region for a passage to the Pacific Ocean.*

Below left: *the official seal of the Merchants of Virginia. Producing enough tobacco and other goods to export to England was a primary goal of the early Virginia settlers.*

Above: *a woodcut shows the shoreline of Virginia, where hundreds of small islands protect the mainland from bad weather and allow for good natural harbors.*

Left: *the seal of the Virginia Company, one of several joint-stock companies formed in England to promote colonization of the American land.*

The settlers then separated into three groups with specific tasks: constructing a fort, planting crops, and further exploring the region. By August, mosquitoes brought an epidemic of malaria, and eight months after their landing, only thirty-eight of the original settlers were alive. Their salvation was due in part to the efforts of Captain John Smith. He negotiated with the Native Americans and persuaded them to trade with the settlers for maize.

The Native American tribes in the region were loosely bound in a confederacy headed by Powhatan. A shrewd leader who mistrusted the English objectives, Powhatan resisted efforts by the English to force the native tribes into a tributary status. Peace was achieved between the English and the Native Americans in later years, but it was not due to the crown's grand scheme to form a partnership. Instead, it was furthered by a marriage between John Rolphe, an English settler, and Pocahontas, Powhatan's daughter.

As accounts of the hardships encountered by the settlers reached England, many financiers of the enterprise realized that much of the difficulty lay in the form of government being imposed in the wilderness region. The original charter had put control of the colony in the hands of the "Council in Virginia," a group of seven men who were accountable to the English government and to the London Company. In 1609 the charter was revised to provide for a governor answerable only to the company.

That year also brought the first women and children to Virginia. Their arrival, together with that of the first black slaves in 1619, marked its transition from trading post to colony. As settlers got control of their own parcels of land, they turned to a new crop that was to be their salvation: a broad-leaved plant, grown by the Indians and refined with West Indian stock, that the world came to know and both love and revile as tobacco. Thanks to tobacco, Virginia attracted labor and capital and became a viable commercial colony. The labor required for the cultivation of tobacco came at first from indentured servants—men and women willing to sell themselves into personal service in return for the price of a passage to Virginia. The problem was that such laborers were white Englishmen who after a fixed period of time, usually seven years, would have to be paid and would change overnight from cheap bound labor to expensive free labor. The importation of black slaves ultimately resolved this difficulty. Yet the purchase price of a good African laborer remained substantially higher than the lease price of a good English servant. The relative price of slaves fell by the end of the seventeenth century because the European slave traders and their African suppliers

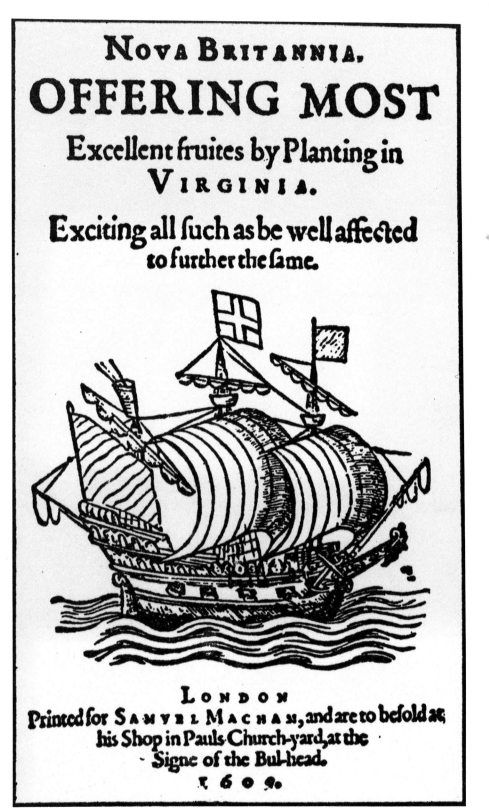

Above: *a pamphlet entitled* Nova Britannia *and published by the London Company promoted colonization in Virginia.*

Above right: *a woodcut of the settlers of Jamestown. The site selected by the settlers was a densely wooded swamp thirty miles up the James River.*

Right: *Virginia settlers under attack by Native Americans. The first English settlement in Virginia, in 1587, ended in the disappearance of 150 settlers.*

were growing more efficient at their unsavory business. In addition, rising life expectancy in the American colonies made it more likely that a planter would in fact get a full lifetime's labor out of a slave who had cost him approximately twice as much up front as an indentured servant.

Economic imperatives pushed Virginia toward a slave society, but conscious political choices made it a free one as well. In 1618 the London Company concluded that the most practical way to govern Virginia was to let the colonists govern themselves. Under the leadership of Governor Edwin Sandys, the company allowed the planters to elect representatives to an assembly, which, together with the governor's council, was empowered to legislate for the colony. The first such assembly, which would be called the House of Burgesses, met in Jamestown in August 1619. Free white males over the age of seventeen elected two representatives from each of

C.Smith taketh the King of Pamavnkee prisoner. -1608.

Left: *a woodcut depicts Captain John Smith's capture of the king of the Pamunkey Indians. Smith devoted much of his energies to effecting a peace between the white settlers and the Native Americans.*

Virginia's eleven towns to it, and it is remembered as the first colonial legislature in the New World. Members of county courts were also chosen to deal with exclusively local affairs.

King James I took control of the colony from the London Company in 1624, and no provision was made for continuing this type of representative arrangement; nor was any forthcoming from his son, the ill-fated Charles I. But as it turned out, the royal governors sent to Virginia by these Stuart kings quickly found that Virginia could best be governed with the aid of Virginians themselves. Given the great distance from the mother country and the fact that the colonists enjoyed all the rights of Englishmen under the common law, there was no holding back the development of a sturdy and resilient tradition of representative government in British North America. The Burgesses began to meet again in 1629, and they have continued to do so annually down to the present day.

A high degree of social stratification characterized this early Southern world. At the bottom labored the

Above: women settlers arrived in Jamestown in 1609. Their arrival, along with that of the first black slaves ten years later, marked the transition of Jamestown from trading post to colony.

black slaves, constituting half the population of Virginia on the eve of the Revolution at about 170,000 souls. Though at the bottom, their influence penetrated all levels, from Africanisms infiltrating the King's English through harsh legal codes. At the top, in baronial splendor and prestige, resided the great planters, who were probably as close as America ever came to a truly European aristocracy. Yet they were different in one respect: in Virginia and the rest of the South, the top echelon was relatively open-ended. New people were always moving up, either through the acquisition of broad acres and troops of slaves or through marriage. In either case, the single prerequisite was land.

It was the yeoman farmer, however, who formed the backbone of society in the early years of the colony. These men possessed small tracts of land, which they worked themselves with the aid of their families and occasionally indentured servants or a few slaves. Poised against the desires and needs of the small farmers were those of the planters. Year after year, the planter class grew in number and strength. While increased taxation and quit-rents and the passage of navigation acts had little impact on the planters, these legal measures were disastrous to the yeoman farmers. Taxes on tobacco rose so high that many indentured servants, once their passage was repaid, migrated to the frontier or to Pennsylvania rather than taking their place as yeoman farmers as their earlier counterparts had done.

Matters came to a head in 1676 when Native Americans stepped up their campaign to rid the western region of Virginia of white settlers. The frontiersmen petitioned the royal governor for help to no avail. Eager to maintain good relations with the Native Americans, and thus safeguard the fur trade, Governor William Berkeley refused to act. Frontiersmen rallied around Nathaniel Bacon, who, although socially and politically was more naturally aligned with the planter class, had holdings on the frontier and was angered over Berkeley's inaction. Bacon, who had been in Virginia for only two years, raised a force of western men and fought the Pamunkeys, the Susquehannocks, and the Occaneechees, despite orders to the contrary from the governor. Bacon and his guards then marched to Jamestown to demand a commission to quell additional Native American tribes along the frontier. In Jamestown, Bacon was arrested but was released on parole. The governor and assembly passed a series of laws, called "Bacon's Laws," aimed at Bacon himself, who had recently been elected to the House of Burgesses. One law prohibited the election to the assembly of anyone who had resided in the colony less than three years or who had been convicted of a "notorious crime."

Bacon returned to the frontier without his desired commission and rallied support for another march to Jamestown. A showdown between the governor and the popular rebel resulted in Berkeley's granting the commission, but shortly thereafter, the governor annulled it. Upon hearing the news that Bacon had been labelled a traitor, his force returned to Jamestown, defeated the governor's militia, and burned the city. A month later, Bacon died from an attack of fever, leaving the revolutionary force without a leader. Berkeley and the assembly wrested control once more, hung two dozen of the mob's leaders, and repealed their earlier slight steps toward more universal white-male suffrage. Of more consequence,

Above: *before long, the Virginia colonists turned to tobacco as a primary crop, and the weed made many planters rich.*

Facing page: *the early years in the Southern colonies were difficult. Here, a man divides among the impoverished settlers kernels of corn for planting.*

however, was the planter class's rejection of the indentured servant system in favor of slavery. Indentured servants could be controlled for only so long as their terms of service, and upon completing their terms they would likely move to the frontier and make costly demands on the colonial government for protection. Slaves, on the other hand, were, in theory, under the planters' perpetual control.

The patterns of settlement and ways of living in the colonial South were as varied as they were elsewhere in North America, and it is wise to remember that "the South" was at no point in its history the great monolith of popular myth. A look at Maryland and the Carolinas brings home two facts vital to the rest of the story: that there are some

things common to life in the South that make it seem very much something of a piece, and that, even so, the South is a very large place and "Southerness" is ever an uneven sort of thing.

Throughout the colonial history of Maryland runs the theme of self-government, the story of a people unwilling to submit to a royal commissioner. Lord Baltimore, a Catholic nobleman, received a grant from the crown to land on the upper Chesapeake, between the Potomac River and the fortieth degree latitude. Maryland, named for the French queen of Charles I, was the first of the great proprietary colonies in America and was intended to serve as a refuge for persecuted Catholics from England. As proprietor, Lord Baltimore had absolute

Above: *the 1634 massacre at Jamestown. Throughout the seventeenth century, relations between the white settlers and the Native Americans were marked by periodic outbursts of violence.*

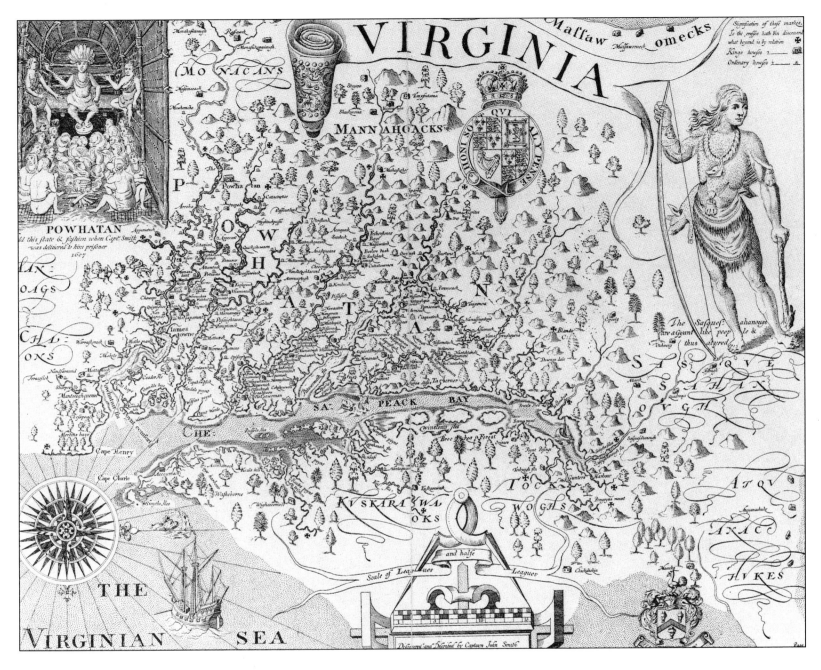

VIRGINIA

POWHATAN
held this state & fashion when Capt. Smith
was delivered to his prisoner
1607

Above: *Captain John Smith's 1612 map of Virginia included the names of the Native American tribes in the area and, in the upper left corner, a depiction of Powhatan, the leader of a loosely bound confederation of native tribes in the Virginia region.*

control over this land. He could enact ordinances, impose punishments for crimes – including the death penalty – and appoint all officials. To enact laws, however, he was required to gain the assent of freemen.

In the fall of 1633, two ships, the *Ark* and the *Dove*, set sail from England to Maryland under the command of Leonard Calvert, brother of the proprietor Lord Baltimore. On board were around two hundred prospective settlers, most of whom were Protestant, not Catholic. By March of 1634, the ships entered the mouth of the Potomac and landed on St. Clement's Island, now called Blakiston Island. Over the next several weeks, the settlers searched for a good site on which to construct their home, chose

the present-day site of St. Mary's, and purchased it from the Yaocomico Indians. Immediately, the settlers, under no special instructions to search for gold or a northwest passage, began clearing land and planting crops.

Lord Baltimore granted more than sixty patents to erect manors, which were planned to serve as judicial centers and the focus of community life. He had difficulty in persuading settlers to become tenants on those manors, however, because so much land was available for purchase in other colonies. Eventually, the manors were carved into many more plantations. As in Virginia, tobacco was the primary crop of the Marylanders. Blessed with a natural setting containing 150 rivers and creeks, residents

on both sides of the Chesapeake Bay constructed hundreds of privately owned wharves. Because Marylanders and northern Virginians were able to ship produce directly to London from these wharves, no major commercial port was established in the colonial period.

Lord Baltimore's insistence on religious toleration encouraged settlement not only by Catholics, but also by other religious faiths. In 1648, a group of Puritans from Virginia, under the leadership of Richard Bennett, decided to leave behind the persecution they suffered under Governor William Berkeley and move to Maryland where Governor William Stone gave them land. These new settlers settled Providence at the present-day site of Annapolis. Located miles away from the colony's governmental center at St. Mary's, the Puritans installed their own local officials and set about directing their own affairs. Lord Baltimore ordered Governor Stone to reassert control over the Puritans, and on March 25, 1655, the Puritan forces and the proprietor's forces met at a battle on the Severn River. The Puritans were victorious and remained out of the reaches of the proprietor's government until 1658. The Puritans continued to stir up trouble over the next fifty years, especially in 1688, when, during the Glorious Revolution, they seized the government. William and Mary made Maryland a royal colony, but in 1715 the fourth Lord Baltimore

Above: *a Native American poses with a keg of tobacco. The native tribes taught the English settlers much about the cultivation of the crop.*

Right: *Jamestown, Virginia, as it appeared in 1622. Built on the lower part of the Chesapeake Bay, Jamestown later became part of the industrial seaboard. Today the Chesapeake Bay region is home to almost 9 million people.*

was regranted rights, and Maryland retained its proprietary form of government until the American Revolution.

In what would become the state of South Carolina, but which was then usually referred to just as "Carolina," we can see in a somewhat different setting some familiar ideals and aspirations that later generations of Southerners fell heir to, for better or worse. Two themes drown out all others. The first is race, or more precisely racial fear. For it was in the rice lands of the South Carolina Low Country that the enslaved blacks vastly outnumbered the whites. The second theme is ruralism, which, like race, shaped the character of colonial South Carolina much as it did that of Virginia. But in South Carolina a different context rendered the otherwise quite ordinary into something peculiar, eccentric, even bizarre. For while most of it was intensely rural, South Carolina also spawned, on the little peninsula between the Ashley and Cooper rivers, what was if not the largest then surely the most glittering of cities anywhere in the Americas. Charleston ruled, literally and figuratively, the vast rural back country whence came much of its wealth.

Settlement in the Carolinas got its start informally in 1653 when settlers from Virginia pushed southward into the area around Albemarle Sound. Eager to escape the taxes and trappings of civilization taking hold in Virginia, these settlers found that life in the region was no more attractive after 1663 when Charles II granted large tracts of land in the Carolinas to eight men who had supported the restoration of the English monarchy.

The eight proprietors were determined to increase the population of their colony and not to depend on refugees from civilized Virginia alone. They promised prospective settlers freedom from customs duties on wine, silk, capers, wax, and other goods shipped from the colony to England for seven years. In addition, they hired John Locke, the noted English philosopher, to aid Sir Anthony Ashley Cooper in drafting a constitution that would be attractive to settlers and at the same time protect the interests of the proprietors. His Fundamental Constitutions reflect a curious vestige of feudalism, including hereditary titles of nobility, along with an innovative republicanism. The proprietors hailed Locke's work but made few efforts to institute the novel form of government. Instead, the government of the Carolinas generally followed the pattern already in place in Virginia.

In 1669, the proprietors agreed to contribute £500 each to a proposed settlement at Port Royal. Three ships sailed from England in August 1660, landing first in Virginia to purchase supplies and then in Barbados to recruit more colonists. That fall, the ships sailed for the Carolinas, but one was wrecked in a gale in the Bahamas. The other two took refuge

Below: the reconstructed Governor's Palace in Colonial Williamsburg, a major outdoor living history site. Leaders in the restoration and re-creation of the site were John D. Rockefeller, Jr., and W. A. R. Goodwin, rector of Bruton Parish Church.

from the storm in Bermuda and after repairs took to the seas again in February 1670. Led by William Sayle, a Puritan settler in the Bahamas and former governor of Bermuda, the group abandoned their plans to land at Port Royal and selected instead a site on the Ashley River. They named their new home Charles Town in honor of the king. Shortly after their landing, the settlers began constructing a new town, which they also called Charles Town, having renamed their original town Kiawah. By the beginning of the 1680s, the new city was home to 1,000 to 1,200 people.

Despite the intention of the proprietors to speed growth in both Upper and Lower Carolina, they generally directed most of their attention to the southern region of the colony, and settlers in the north were dissatisfied. Governors were deposed, and settlers made direct appeals to the crown. In 1719 the Carolinas' petition to be made a royal colony was granted, and eight years later Parliament divided the region and made North Carolina a separate royal colony.

The differences in the two colonies ran deep. North Carolina had been settled as early as 1653, ten years before Charles II granted land to the proprietors. Many of the first settlers had completed terms as indentured servants and were eager to grab bits of land for themselves, and ever-increasing numbers of new settlers were attracted by laws that forbade suits over debts incurred before settlers moved to the region and that exempted them from taxes for one year.

Tobacco became the primary crop of North Carolinians, but because of the area's treacherous shoreline, the settlers found it difficult to move their produce to market. Generally, they were forced to haul their crops overland to Virginia where government agents imposed importation taxes. As a result, North Carolina remained a country of small farms where subsistence rather than trade was the rule.

South Carolina, on the other hand, became a region of great plantations growing easily marketed crops: rice and indigo. By the 1730s, the commercial possibilities of rice culture were being realized on a large scale all up and down the tidal and inland swamplands of the Low Country. Indigo, a plant grown for the rich blue dye it yielded, thrived on the drier soils unsuitable for rice, and thus ideally complemented it. Nor did indigo require attention

Left: *a view of the reconstructed Capitol in Colonial Williamsburg. The original building was constructed in 1705.*

Williamsburg's preservation and re-creation began in 1928. Today about a million visitors stroll along its streets each year.

in the winter, which left the slave labor force available for other tasks.

Within a few years of the establishment of the first rice plantations in South Carolina at the end of the seventeenth century, the black population was greater than the white. Laborers died quickly in the malarial conditions of the swamplands, but planters grew rich and replaced their dead and sick workers with an ever-increasing number of black slaves. Owners of the sprawling plantations often lived in Charleston and left the management of the lands and workforce in the hands of overseers. As a result, slave codes in the rice colonies were more strict than those instituted elsewhere. The government placed no restriction on how a master might treat his slaves, however, as they were considered to be his absolute property. Cruel punishment was inflicted on many South Carolina slaves for minor infractions, and overseers were generally more concerned over

commissions they received for harvests than over the health and welfare of the workforce.

Between 1740 and the Revolution – the golden age of colonial South Carolina – prices rose and planters expanded production. Rice exports tripled, those of indigo quadrupled, and the annual value of these crops soared five times over. Everywhere planters prospered, many to a degree that would never be known again in the South. Far more than was the case with tobacco, both of South Carolina's great crops were well suited to large-scale farming units, which meant that even though South Carolina was a much younger colony than Virginia, its plantation system, which was utterly dependent on slave labor, sunk roots fast and deep. Not all the rice plantations were grand estates; the average plantation probably counted 300-500 acres worked by a dozen or so slaves. But rice culture was expensive and capital-intensive, which encouraged engrossment

Above: *Virginia's House of Burgesses first met in Williamsburg in 1629, beginning a democratic tradition that has continued until today.*

Right: *a portrait of William Byrd, II, by Sir Godfrey Kneller. Educated in England, Byrd returned to Virginia to manage the plantations he inherited from his father, Colonel William Byrd. He enlarged the family home, Westover, and compiled one of the largest libraries in the colonies.*

TO BE SOLD, on board the Ship *Bance Island*, on tuesday the 6th of *May* next, at *Ashley-Ferry*; a choice cargo of about 250 fine healthy

NEGROES, juſt arrived from the Windward & Rice Coaſt. —The utmoſt care has already been taken, and ſhall be continued, to keep them free from the leaſt danger of being infected with the SMALL-POX, no boat having been on board, and all other communication with people from *Charles-Town* prevented.

Auſtin, Laurens, & Appleby.

N. B. Full one Half of the above Negroes have had the SMALL-POX in their own Country.

Far left: *the Westover Plantation on the James River, near Charles City, Virginia. The plantation was home to Colonel William Byrd, I (1652-1704) and his son William Byrd, II (1674-1744).*

Left: *an advertisment announcing the arrival of black slaves in the colonies. The writer of this copy took care to inform potential purchasers that the blacks on board the ships had either not been exposed to smallpox or had already had the disease in their own country.*

of the best lands by the wealthiest planters.

In South Carolina, the white planters took to themselves everything they could imagine of aristocracy, and they gave to their new native land a patina it has not lost in the centuries since. Not every white lived like a grandee, but many of the wealthy, haughty Low Country planters not only ruled South Carolina but supplied its culture with a mold and a standard of aspiration. History proved their strength when, even after there had grown up in the South in the antebellum era a substantial and genuine middle class – independent people, neither rich nor poor, but ever jealous of their freedoms – observers still remarked about the pervasive influence of the planter class. While the planters never ruled the larger South in years to come as indisputably as they did colonial South Carolina, their presence and way of life unquestionably set the tone and defined the goals for much of Southern culture right up until the Civil War laid to waste that remote, peculiar civilization.

The last English colony in America, Georgia was also the only colony that formed the focus of a political and social experiment. General James Oglethorpe was concerned over protecting his interests in a rice company in South Carolina where attacks by the Spanish from Florida were common.

He was perhaps no less concerned over the insidious conditions in English debtors' prisons. His two interests coalesced in a scheme to establish a new colony that would serve as a buffer between South Carolina and Florida and would be settled by former debtors' prison inmates who would repay their debts through military service. Parliament approved the plan and granted to a group of philanthropists the right to establish the colony of Georgia. These proprietors were to govern and supervise the colony for twenty-one years and then return it to the hands of the crown.

The first group of settlers (130 men, women, and children) arrived at the mouth of the Savannah River in the spring of 1733. General Oglethorpe laid out the city of Savannah almost immediately, and over the next six years, nearly five thousand immigrants from Salzburg, Scotland and Moravia joined the original group. The proprietors allotted fifty-acre tracts of land to settlers in exchange for military service. From the colony's founding, Parliament had banned the importation or use of slaves in the region because of fears that the slaves would aid the Spanish in any hostilities that occurred. To help the settlers in farming, the proprietors encouraged indentured servitude, but the costs were too high for many

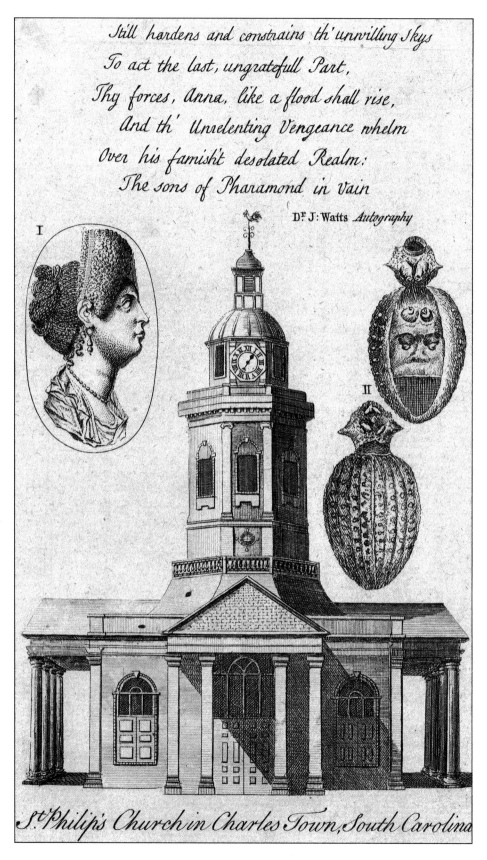

Still hardens and constrains th'unwilling Skys
To act the last, ungratefull Part,
Thy forces, Anna, like a flood shall rise,
And th' Unrelenting Vengeance whelm
Over his famish't desolated Realm:
The sons of Pharamond in vain

Dr J: Watts *Autography*

St Philip's Church in Charles Town, South Carolina

Above: *a copper engraving of St. Philip's Church in Charles Town, South Carolina. Within ten years of its founding, the city grew to a population of more than 1,000 people.*

settlers. They envied the large plantations and slave holdings of their neighbors in South Carolina, and only seven years after Georgia's founding, they began to ignore the law banning slavery. By the end of the 1740s, the law was repealed, and the plantation system gained a strong hold in the colony.

The colonies had been established under various circumstances; Virginia had been settled as an English trading post and North Carolina's first settlers were refugees from civilization and taxes in Virginia. Many of South Carolina's first families were recruited in Barbados, and lived under the ineffective rule of their King's appointees. Only Georgia began its existence as a social and military experiment. Along the colonies' frontiers at the Appalachian Mountains and beyond there was still another form of settlement though.

Interest in western lands began as early as 1650 when Captain Abraham Wood led an expedition through the Blue Ridge Mountains to the falls of the Roanoke River. Over the next fifty years, many Virginians made fortunes in the fur trade in the west, reaching as far as the Tennessee Valley. In 1716, Virginia's governor Alexander Spotswood led a group of explorers into the Valley of Virginia, returned to Williamsburg, and petitioned the crown for grants of land in the western territory.

Joining the Tidewater emigrés were settlers from Pennsylvania, whose colonial government encouraged individuals who had completed terms as indentured servants to move south. The first settlers moved to areas around Martinsburg and Shepherdstown in what is now West Virginia and to the region around Winchester, Virginia, in 1726. Within only eight years, the Virginia colonial government organized Orange County to impose a governmental system on the new western settlements, and four years after that the districts of Frederick and Augusta were established. Farther west, the region that encompasses the present-day states of West Virginia, Kentucky, Ohio, Indiana, Illinois, Michigan, and Wisconsin was named West Augusta.

North Carolina's western region filled up with Scotch-Irish and Germans from Virginia, and six counties were formed between 1743 and 1762. South Carolina's western lands were parcelled out to prospective settlers who also received livestock and supplies from the colonial government. Both Georgia and Maryland priced western lands cheaply.

The western settlers were of a different temperament than the Tidewater settlers, and their surroundings imposed a contrasting lifestyle. Because of the difficulty of moving their produce to markets, the western settlers generally operated small farms not dependent on slave labor.

While immigrants from the Middle Atlantic states

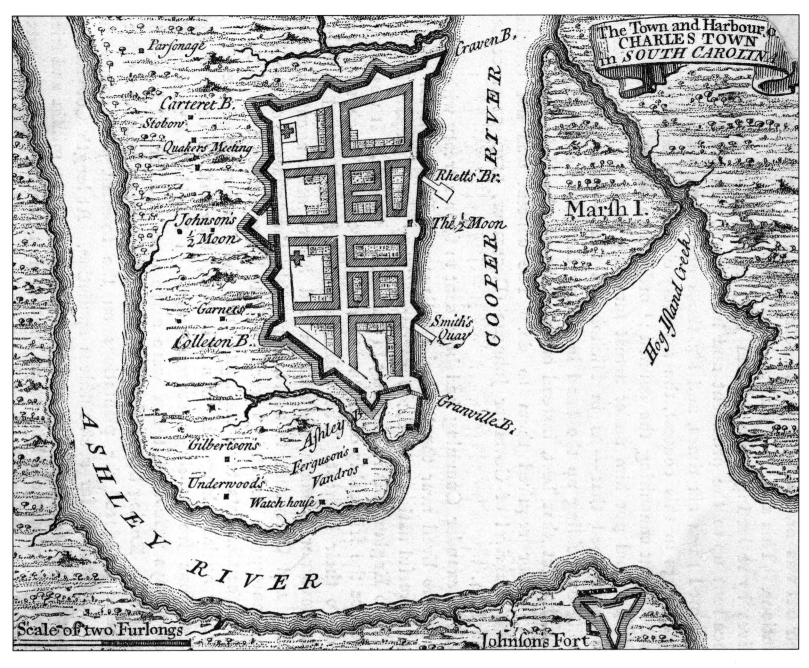

poured into the South's frontier, planters from the Tidewater region began to acquire huge tracts of western lands through royal land grants. They formed land companies and outfitted prospective settlers moving west. George Washington began his career as a surveyor hired by Lord Fairfax in 1748 to chart lands between the Potomac and Rappahannock rivers. Other members of the Washington family – Lawrence and Augustine – along with leading families in Virginia – the Lees and the Dinwiddies – formed the Ohio Land Company and received a grant of 500,000 acres along the Ohio River between the Monongahela and the Little Kanawha. Other land companies, including the Loyal Land Company and the Greenbrier Company, received lands in western Virginia and North Carolina.

The problem with this full-scale land speculation was that the territories the English colonists were granted were claimed by the French. Eager to maintain control of the region, the governor of New France sent Celonron de Blainville to the Ohio Valley to garner Indian support and install lead plates denoting France's possessions all along the Ohio River. The next governor, the Marquis de Duquesne, ordered a series of forts to be constructed from Lake Erie south along the Ohio River.

Meanwhile, Virginia land companies pushed to the west and attempted to gain land concessions from the Iroquois. In 1753, Governor Dinwiddie of Virginia sent George Washington into the Ohio Valley

Above: *a map of the town and harbor of Charles Town, South Carolina, at the meeting of the Ashley and Cooper rivers. The town was the most important port in the South, and between 1740 and 1773, five companies established shipyards there. Renamed Charleston in 1818, the city is today the thirteenth largest port in the United States.*

A

DISCOURSE

Concerning the defign'd

ESTABLISHMENT

Of a New

COLONY

TO THE

South of *Carolina,*

IN THE

Moft delightful Country of the Universe.

By Sir ROBERT MOUNTGOMERY, *Baronet.*

LONDON:

Printed in the Year. 1717.

Above: *Sir Robert Mountgomery's 1717 pamphlet describing the establishment of the colony of South Carolina.*

Facing page left: *T. A. Gent's 1682 pamphlet on the Carolinas promoted the "healthfulness of the air," and the "pleasantness of the place."*

Facing page, right: *a copper engraving of The Indigo Manufactory, originally published in Middleton's Complete System of Geography (1779).*

to warn the French that they were trespassing. The French refused to leave their forts, however, and the following year the Virginia colony sent a regiment commanded by Washington and Joshua Fry to eject the French by force. The Virginia regiment attacked the French at Great Meadows of the Youghiogheny in western Pennsylvania. The French counterattacked at Fort Necessity, forcing Washington to withdraw on July 5.

Parliament then dispatched Edward Braddock to America to serve as commander of all British forces in the colonies, which included two Irish regiments and colonial forces. While the colonies acceded to the crown's directive to provide funds to Braddock to wage war against the French and their Indian allies, they did so reluctantly. Braddock's concentration on routing the French from the northern region left the western frontiers of the Southern colonies without protection. Governor Dinwiddie authorized the raising of regiments under George Washington, who was appointed "Colonel of the Virginia Regiment." In addition, the Virginia assembly authorized funds to be used to construct a string of forts from Hampshire County to Halifax County. In 1756 alone, Washington directed the construction of eighty-one forts, which housed not only the military but also local homestead families whenever the Native Americans posed particularly frightening threats.

North Carolina Governor Dobbs also authorized the building of a fort on the South Yadkin River for troops under Captain Hugh Waddell. Fort Dobbs, near Statesville, provided the only haven for North Carolina frontier families. South Carolinians faced raids from the Cherokees, and there the colonial government erected Fort Loudon to protect Charleston. Because of the success of the troops stationed in this southern string of forts, most of the fighting in the French and Indian War, which lasted until 1763, took place in the north.

Despite the king's proclamation that year that all lands beyond the Alleghenies were to be preserved for the Indians, land speculation in the west continued. Settlements sprang up at Charleston, Morgantown, Buckhannon, and Wheeling in present-day West Virginia. To the south, other Virginians and North Carolinians settled in the Watauga country, which at the time of their move to the region, they believed was part of Virginia. The settlers, including James Robertson and John Sevier, requested protection from North Carolina when they discovered their error, but when the government failed to recognize their request speedily, they organized the Watauga Association and formed their own government. At first they leased land from the Indians, but by 1775 they secured a permanent transfer. Three years later,

CAROLINA;

OR A

DESCRIPTION

Of the PRESENT STATE of that

COUNTRY,

AND

The *Natural Excellencies* thereof, *viz.* The *Healthfulneſs* of the *Air*, Pleaſantneſs of the Place, Advantage and Uſefulneſs of thoſe Rich Commodities there plentifully abounding, which much encreaſe and flouriſh by the Induſtry of the *Planters* that daily enlarge that *Colony.*

Publiſhed by **T. A.** Gent.

Clerk on Board his Majeſties Ship the *Richmond*, which was ſent out in the Year 1680. with particular Inſtructions to enquire into the State of that Country, by His Majeſties Special Command, and Return'd this Preſent Year, 1682.

L O N D O N,

Printed for *W. C.* and to be Sold by Mrs. *Grover* in *Pelican Court* in *Little Britain,* 1682.

Engraved for Middleton's Complete System of Geography.

THE INDIGO MANUFACTORY

1 Vat. 2 Pounding Tub. 3 Receiver. 4 The Water filtrating from the Indigo. 5 Indigo Plants. 6 Indians carrying D.º in Sacks 7 Drying Cases. 8 Indians carrying Indigo to the drying Cases.

North Carolina reorganized the territory into the Washington District.

Daniel Boone began his famous explorations and hunting expeditions in Kentucky in 1769. Returning to North Carolina in 1771, he enticed Richard Henderson to finance an expedition and settlement in Kentucky. The Transylvania Land Company, including Henderson, John Sevier, James Robertson, and Isaac Shelby, persuaded the Cherokee to sell all of Kentucky and part of Tennessee for £10,000 worth of goods. While the land company negotiated with the Cherokee, Boone and a group of settlers chopped their way through the wilderness to found Boonesborough. Henderson's plan was to unite the new settlement with two older ones at Harrodsburg and St. Asaphs under a single legislature of Transylvania. In 1776, the Kentucky settlements were incorporated into Kentucky County, Virginia.

A company formed by Pennsylvanians, New Yorkers, and Virginians petitioned the crown for rights to establish a colony south of the Ohio River and east of the Little Kanawha River. By 1772, the charter for Vandalia was submitted for approval, but before the charter was approved, the colonies and their mother country were embroiled in the Revolutionary War.

THE SOUTH AND A NEW NATION

By the eve of the Revolutionary War, the South had evolved into an established rural society the prosperity of which rested on plantation-based, staple crop agriculture and subsistence farming. In 1763, the year generally regarded as the end of the Colonial period and the beginning of the Revolutionary, the South was inhabited by 700,00 people, excluding the Native Americans. Basically of English descent, the white population carried on their cultural traditions in the face of more recent arrivals of Germans, Roman Catholic Irish, Scots-Irish, and French Huguenots.

The population in the South included about 300,000 black slaves – approximately two-fifths of the total. A large number of slaves were American-born, but the slave trade continued. Virginia had more slaves than any other colony – about 100,000 in 1763. About 50,000 slaves lived in North Carolina, 50,000 in Maryland, 70,000 in South Carolina, and 50,000 in Georgia. These slaves manned the plantations, raising the great staple crops of tobacco, rice, and indigo for export. As an economic institution and as a system of racial control, slavery defined relations between black and white. Racial prejudice came to these shores with the Europeans, and in the eighteenth century abstract questions about the morality of slavery were, in the face of that institution's indisputable economic utility, kept muffled and largely private. On the eve of the Revolution, slavery was practiced in the Northern colonies as well, though nowhere north of the Potomac did blacks constitute anything approaching forty percent of the population, as they did in Virginia and in most other Southern colonies, to say nothing of the sixty-six percent in South Carolina.

The war by which America became one nation was fought between 1775 and 1781 up and down the

Left: *Monticello in Virginia was home to Thomas Jefferson. Built to his own design, it was purchased by The Thomas Jefferson Memorial Foundation in 1923, and subsequently restored.*

English colonies from New England to Georgia. Southerners and Northerners shed blood equally to throw off the British yoke; the leader of their armies, George Washington, was a Virginian and a slaveholder. The war began on Northern soil at Lexington and Concord in Massachusetts. It ended on Southern soil, on the Yorktown Peninsula in Virginia, only a few miles from Jamestown and Williamsburg.

The break with England came slowly and was the result of changing conditions within the British Empire and of the attempts of the British Parliament to raise new revenues in the colonies. Trouble brewed throughout the 1760s and into the early 1770s as Britain strove to recover from her costly victory over France in the Seven Years' War and to maintain a standing army of sixteen regiments in North America and the British West Indies. With the passage of the Stamp Act and the Sugar Act, however, trouble flared openly.

The colonists had petitioned Parliament about the new taxes, but little attention had been paid the complaints. In Virginia, however, the complaints turned into political action. The House of Burgesses was meeting in Williamsburg when word came that the Stamp Act had passed. As the session came to a close, all but thirty-nine of the 116 members returned home. Then on May 29, Patrick Henry, who had been a member of the Burgesses for only nine days, secured the passage of five resolutions against Parliament's treatment of the colonies. Older members fought against Henry's resolutions, possibly because they were unwilling to stir up more trouble after their petitions of the preceding fall, or perhaps because they wanted to find out how the other colonies would react to the Stamp Act before they themselves took steps to condemn it.

Henry's resolutions set forth in bold language the rights of the colonists as Englishmen and the principle of taxation only with proper representation. The fifth resolve, passing by a margin of twenty to nineteen, declared that the colony's assembly alone had the right to levy taxes. On June 1, the lieutenant governor of the colony, Frances Fauquier, dissolved the House of Burgesses, despite the fact that the house had repealed the revolutionary fifth resolve the previous day.

To the north, legislatures in other colonies – Massachusetts, Connecticut, and Rhode Island – condemned the Stamp Act, and on June 8, Massachusetts extended an invitation to all other colonies to send delegates to a Stamp Act Congress. When Parliament again refused to heed the petitions for repeal of the act, colonists throughout the South and North rebelled by attacking stamp masters, destroying the stamps, and conducting business without purchasing the official stamps.

In Maryland, the protest against the Stamp Act took place initially outside the realm of the legislature. The stamp master in Maryland, Zachariah Hood, returned to his home in Annapolis from a visit to London in August 1765. Stirred to anger by articles in the *Maryland Gazette*, Marylanders met Hood at the dock to prevent his landing and whipped, hanged, and burned his effigy. Hood eventually fled the colony and resigned as stamp master.

Maryland's Assembly convened in September 1765, for the first time since November 1763, to draft resolves against the Stamp Act and select representatives to the Stamp Act Congress. From the ranks of Maryland's wealthiest class came a persuasive polemicist: Daniel Dulaney. This prosperous citizen clearly delineated the argument that Parliament had no power to impose taxes on the

Above: *Virginian George Washington served as the commander of the American forces during the Revolutionary War and was elected first president of the new United States.*

Right: *Thomas Jefferson succeeded John Adams as president of the United States in 1801. As president, Jefferson angered many of his supporters by refusing to adhere to a strict interpretation of federal power as defined by the Constitution.*

colonists and blasted the theory that the Americans were "virtually" represented in Parliament. His *Considerations on the Propriety of Imposing Taxes in the British Colonies, for the purpose of raising a Revenue, by Act of Parliament* was well received throughout the thirteen colonies.

In North Carolina, the lower house of the assembly had wrested much power from the crown's appointed officials since North Carolina became a separate royal colony in 1729, and it was one of two colonial legislatures to declare the Stamp Act unconstitutional even before it was passed. Although the North Carolina Assembly was not in session when word of the Stamp Act's passage reached America, colonists held meetings throughout the summer and early fall. In Cross Creek, Edenton, New Bern, and Wilmington, they pledged to refrain from using the stamps. Governor William Tryon attempted to appease the North Carolinians, offering to pay for the stamps needed by his office out of his personal funds. He also tried to lure the colony's wealthiest men into accepting the tax by hinting that North Carolina would reap the benefits of trade

discontinued in colonies that flouted the law. His enticements fell on deaf ears. North Carolina would have no part of the hated tax. The governor, the courts, and the customs officials then halted business and judicial affairs until the colonists submitted. In addition, a British naval captain, Jacob Lobb, seized three ships in the Cape Fear River that lacked stamped papers.

In Wilmington, hundreds of colonists gathered to condemn the tax and the seizure of the ships and to demand that the port of Brunswick be reopened. As they marched toward Brunswick, their ranks grew to more than a thousand angry, armed men. On February 20, Captain Lobb gave in to the mob, some of whom had occupied Fort Johnston, and custom officials promised to take no further steps to enforce the Stamp Act.

In South Carolina, an angry mob thronged through the streets of Charleston in October as word spread that the stamps had reached the harbor. An effigy of a stamp master in gallows was placed in the city, and crowds gathered about it. The colonists then undertook to ferret out the stamps. They ransacked

Above left: *John Adams was the second president of the United States, and during his administration his own political party, the Federalists, lost ground against the growing Republican Party of Thomas Jefferson.*

Above: *an architectural drawing of Thomas Jefferson's home, Monticello, which was designed by Jefferson himself.*

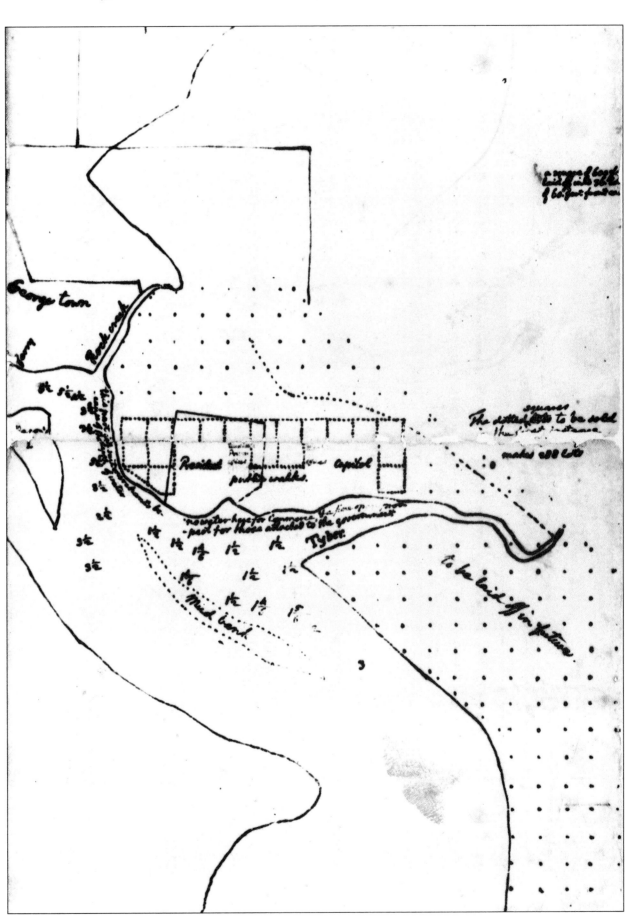

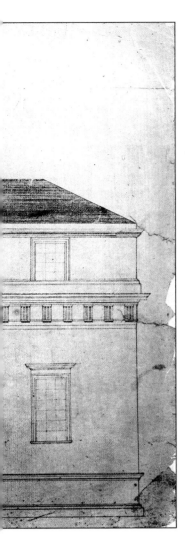

Right: *Thomas Jefferson's 1791 sketch of Washington, D.C. Land for the new capital city was set aside by both Virginia and Maryland. Jefferson's design included sites for the capitol building, the presidential home, and public walks.*

Left: *Edmund Randolph served in the Virginia Convention of 1776 and as attorney-general of Virginia before his twenty-fifth birthday. He also served as attorney-general of the United States under George Washington.*

Below left: *Thomas Jefferson faced strong opposition both from the Federalists and members of his own Republican Party when he attempted to strengthen the federal government.*

the home of George Saxby, stamp inspector, and searched the home of Henry Laurens before William Bull II, the lieutenant governor, announced that the stamps had been secured in Fort Johnson. Saxby and Caleb Lloyd then declared they would refrain from enforcing the Stamp Act until Parliament had time to reconsider the measure.

Despite the usual efforts to oppose the enforcement of the Stamp Act – the burning of effigies, gathering of mobs, and demands to stamp masters to resign their commissions – Georgians eventually submitted to the law, due in part to the efforts of Governor James Wright. In the colonies of East and West Florida as well, the colonists gave in to their governors' demands for enforcement.

The period of enforcement, however, was brief. In March 1766, Parliament repealed the measure. Several factors came to play in the repeal, chief

among them the fact that Britain, still suffering under economic depression, had lost trade through American boycotts of goods and had lost repayment of debts owed by the Americans to British merchants.

After the Stamp Act crisis Parliament came under the powerful sway of Charles Townshend, chancellor of the exchequer, who devised new means of raising money in the colonies to pay for a portion of the large British army stationed there. Duties were proposed on paint, glass, paper, and tea imported by the colonies. In the South, reaction against the Townshend duties was slow in gathering steam. Most merchants in the region were factors of British companies and thus had little at stake financially. Planters and farmers, too, were little affected by the duties. As Samuel Adams and the Massachusetts House of Representatives distributed their Circular Letter, resistance in the South picked up momentum. Virginia

planters, with the approval of the Burgesses, petitioned the King and Parliament and condemned the import duties as unconstitutional. The lower house of Maryland's legislature, ignoring threats of disbanding by the governor, also petitioned the King, as did those in South Carolina, Georgia, and North Carolina. Eventually, Townshend's successor, Frederick, Lord North, repealed the duties, except for those on tea. Troops remained in Boston to quell any signs of rebellion, and in the charged atmosphere, violence broke out on March 5, 1770. News of the Boston Massacre spread quickly, but it was coupled with news of the repeal of the Townshend duties. Most colonists believed they had won a crucial battle against Britain, and over the next three years, the colonists were generally determined to avoid further trouble.

The fall of 1773 brought new contention, however, again with tea at its crux. Parliament had granted the East India Company a monopoly in the tea trade in the colonies and had designated tea traders in each of the colonies to handle distribution. Boston's famous "Tea Party" has outshone the rebellions in other colonies over the years, but events in South Carolina were no less important. Determined to prevent the sale of the East India Company's tea in Charleston, colonists attended two mass meetings in the city in December 1773. They demanded that the ship loaded with tea in Charleston's harbor return to Britain with its cargo intact. The ship remained in the harbor, and on December 22, growing concerned over the security of the ship, customs officials removed the tea to a public warehouse where it remained unsold.

To punish the rebellious colony of Massachusetts after the Tea Party and provide an example to other colonies, Parliament passed the Coercive Acts. Combined with a new Quartering Act and the Quebec Act, which threatened the colonies' jurisdictions to the west, the punitive measures fed the flames of rebellion. In Virginia, the House of Burgesses declared a day of fasting and prayer on June 1, the day on which the Boston port was to be closed by the Coercive Acts. Lord Dunmore dissolved the house, and its members gathered at Raleigh Tavern in Williamsburg. There they called for a Continental Congress and stated that if the "Intolerable" Acts were not repealed by August 10, 1775, the Virginia colony would halt all exports to Britain.

The delegates to the First Continental Congress, including twenty men from the South, drew up a Declaration of Rights at the September 1775 meeting in Philadelphia. Urging the repeal of all the laws they deemed unconstitutional, the delegates called for nonconsumption of all British goods after December 1 and an embargo on shipments to Britain after September 10. The sole exception to the embargo

was rice. South Carolina delegates had pressed for the exception because by law, their rice could be sold only to Britain. An embargo on rice would damage the colony's economy more than embargoes on products of other colonists, who were allowed to sell their crops and manufactures elsewhere.

After the First Continental Congress events smoldered while the British hesitated to commit the troops necessary to enforce the Parliamentary will, and the colonists hesitated to provoke the final break. Violence finally came in April 1775 at Lexington and Concord near Boston. The civil authority of the

Crown disintegrated throughout the colonies as the royal governors were besieged and the colonial assemblies began to act as independent governments. The Second Continental Congress convened in May 1775, but unlike earlier inter-colonial gatherings, this was not merely an angry debating society aiming to compile a list of grievances against England or to issue statements about the sacred rights of Englishmen. While there was still no formal split with England, the Congress began to do things that proper, constituted governments do. George Washington was appointed military commander in

Above: *a street scene in New Orleans, Louisiana. One of the many actions taken by President Thomas Jefferson that riled his Republican supporters was his purchase of the Louisiana territory, a purchase that nearly*

doubled the size of the United States. Costing about $15 million, the new territory was home to some 50,000 people, who became citizens of the United States by executive act after the purchase was completed by treaty in May 1802.

chief (a move that firmly bound the Southern colonists to the Revolution), the printing of paper money was authorized and emissaries were dispatched to foreign governments to explore the prospects for military assistance. The Congress also petitioned George III one final time for redress and, for their trouble, were rebuffed with the royal declaration that the colonies were in a state of rebellion and with the dispatch of 25,000 troops.

Sentiment in America in favor of actual separation grew quickly, and by the spring of 1776 the colonial assemblies began to reconstitute themselves as sovereign governments of independent states and to instruct their delegates to the Continental Congress sitting in Philadelphia to vote out a resolution of independence. In June 1776, in response to the welling up of this feeling, a Virginian, Richard Henry Lee, introduced the ice-breaking, and treasonous, motion that "the United Colonies are, and of right ought to be, free and independent states." The Congress passed it on July 2, and with that, from the American point of view, anyway, independence was asserted – rather than on July 4 when Thomas Jefferson's, Benjamin Franklin's, and John Adams's more famous

declaration was approved. That document, which had been much worked over, artfully combined two things. The first was a point-by-point indictment of the tyrannies that George III had allegedly wrought on the colonies; the second was a tight and cogent exposition of John Locke's theory of the social contract, a statement of the inviolable natural rights of free men, and the assertion of the right of a people to change their government. The impact of the Revolution in the South, as in the other former colonies, was primarily political; heads did not roll, and the social order was not upended. The words and deeds of men from the Southern colonies spoke loudly and memorably – Patrick Henry, Richard Henry Lee, Thomas Jefferson, George Washington – and there is no doubt that the war experience helped mold the beginnings of a first South. Southern leadership came essentially from the plantation aristocracy. Tories, that is, supporters of Great Britain, were weak in Virginia and Maryland, about evenly balanced with Revolutionary forces in North and South Carolina, and probably in the majority in Georgia. But most of the Southern aristocracy favored independence, and these were the people who continued to exercise power after the war.

In the wake of independence, all the states drew up constitutions, reducing the powers of the governors, who had been royal appointees, but none granted universal male suffrage. Virginia, Maryland, and North Carolina wrote bills of rights guaranteeing trial by jury, freedom of speech, and religious toleration. In South Carolina and Georgia, those rights were confirmed in the states' constitutions themselves. The Church of England was disestablished everywhere, but efforts to create public schools failed. Most Southern states began to abolish the slave trade, but not slavery itself. Many planters felt that the existing order depended on the continuation of a massive black labor force and thus, necessarily, of slavery, and while there was genuine moral aversion to the institution inside the South, it was usually coupled with the conviction that emancipation was unthinkable without colonization of the blacks outside North America.

As the states emerged from war with a great world power, there was much to bind them together despite themselves. They had a common enemy and felt a healthy fear of further British aggression long into the post-war period. The war had enlisted men in a common army, and most of the prominent Southern soldiers of the Revolution remained devoted nationalists until their deaths. Similar if not identical ethnic backgrounds, cultural habits, and environment, together with a single language engendered a common feeling that, properly nurtured and politically cultivated, might grow to

Above: *John C. Calhoun, vice-president in Andrew Jackson's administration, and ardent supporter of state's rights.*

Facing page: *Washington, Henry, and Pendleton leave Washington's home, Mount Vernon, to attend the First Continental Congress.*

nationalism. Sectional divisiveness stemmed from economic and political conflicts that became more apparent as nationalism grew. Could the more populous North, progressively turning toward commerce and manufacturing, coexist contentedly with a staunchly agricultural South? Would their divergent demands on the new national state prove too much for even the best of constitutions to contain? On the other hand, would the differences between the sections make them the perfectly complementary parts of a single whole? The outcome depended on whether the new nation could be constructed skillfully enough to accommodate unplanned-for eventualities in such a vast and loosely knit territory. The first attempt at such a construction, the Articles of Confederation, left something to be desired in this regard; the second, the Constitution of 1787, brilliantly conceived as it was, also barely met the test, and ultimately it took a horrific civil war to confirm and make permanent its principles.

Southern nationalists played an important role in moving America toward a stronger form of government than the Articles of Confederation had

Juſt Imported in the ſhip GRANBY, JOSEPH BLEWER Maſter,

Seventy *Gold-Coaſt* SLAVES

of variouſages, and both ſexes,
To be ſold on board ſaid ſhip at Mr. Plumſted's wharf, by
WILLING and *MORRIS*,
And a part of them are intended to be ſent in a few days to Dock Creek, there to be ſold, by Mr. Thomas Mudock for caſh or country produce,

SLAVERY ADVERTISEMENT.

Above: *an advertisment announces the arrival of seventy slaves from the Gold Coast of Africa. The sale was scheduled to take place on board the ship* Granby *at the wharf of a Mr. Plumsted.*

Below: *Richmond was founded at the falls of the James River in 1733 and later became the capital of the state of Virginia.*

Right: *many of the first slaves brought to the United States were first taken to the West Indies. Those not sold there were shipped to Charleston, which became a base for intercoastal trade.*

offered. They feared both the domestic turbulence of the Confederation period and foreign intervention in a fledgling country too weak to protect itself. They believed in republican, though not necessarily democratic, government and in the reality of complementary sectional economies. To many of them it seemed that the South held a commanding geographical position with respect to westward expansion and so was destined to become the most powerful part of the new nation. In the summer of 1787 a Constitutional Convention was held in Philadelphia to draft a new fundamental law for America. Southern delegates were mostly propertied aristocrats who favored radical change to relieve the weaknesses of the Confederation, which had failed to protect property and to establish a working republic. The Virginia delegation was headed by George Washington himself, an ardent nationalist who deplored sectionalism. He was joined by James Madison; scholar, politician, planter, and future leading philosopher of the Constitution. Madison deplored the Confederation's lack of a president and a judiciary and the general absence of strong central government, and even as he sought a radical cure, he epitomized the rift in the Southern psyche with regard to constitutional government.

On one hand, a strong central authority seemed a good and necessary thing. On the other, its existence would require protections: guarantees that the interests of the Southern states would not be endangered by a self-aggrandizing central power. Madison realized that the true rift at the convention was not between the large states and the small ones, as many believed, but between the Northern and the Southern states. George Mason, his fellow Virginian, was more suspicious and feared that a strong central government would inevitably threaten civil liberty and republicanism, and that the commercial economy of the North would one day overpower the agricultural South. Two presidents, he said, each with an absolute veto, were the only way to protect the interests of his section. There were two conspicuous Virginia absentees: Thomas Jefferson, who was serving as the American minister in Paris, and Patrick Henry, who said he smelled the rat of central government and stayed away. Pierce Butler, from North Carolina, was probably the strongest defender of the slaveholding interest at the convention, taking the position that the interests of the North and the South were as different as those of Russia and Turkey.

The division between large states and small ones over equality of representation in the new national legislature was closed by the compromise that gave all states, whatever their population, an equal voice – two seats – in the Senate. But the deeper and more

Above: *Charleston, South Carolina, in 1780. By the end of the Revolutionary War, Charleston was a major city, rivaling New York and Liverpool as an international center of trade.*

Left: *Andrew Jackson from Tennessee was elected president in 1828. He first drew national attention during the War of 1812 at the Battle of New Orleans.*

Right: *slavery continued to be a major component of the sectionalist debate, but equally important in the early national period were arguments over protective tariffs. The industrial North favored tariffs; the agricultural South opposed them because they raised the prices of the goods Southerners had to purchase from outside their own region.*

enduring division between Northern and Southern states centered on the perception of their conflicting economic systems and ran to hard questions about the control of taxation, foreign commerce, and the slave trade. Compromises were worked out, not all of which stood the test of time. The "three-fifths" compromise established the "Federal Ratio," by which three-fifths of the slave population would be counted for purposes of both representation and taxation. The Southern states opposed taxes on exports and wanted a two-thirds vote to be necessary for the levying of import tariffs; the compromise indeed banned export duties but made it possible to establish an import tariff with a simple majority. Little was said about slavery on moral grounds, and no effort was made at abolition, which would probably have jeopardized the whole convention.

Opposition to ratification was generally stronger in the South than in the North, and the state-by-state debates foreshadowed the sectional arguments that would be heard many years later. Georgia, fearful of Spanish incursions and Indian attacks, ratified the Constitution unanimously. North Carolina voted 184 to 84 to withhold ratification until a bill of rights was added. In South Carolina, opponents feared that Northern majorities would inevitably oppress the South, while proponents claimed the concessions made in Philadelphia were only minor and pointed to the system of checks and balances that would, they said, adequately protect Southern interests. Opponents extracted the agreement that the South Carolina delegation in Philadelphia would support amendments protecting both civil liberties and states' rights, and in the subsequent Tenth Amendment all powers not expressly granted to the central government were reserved for the states. In Virginia, Patrick Henry stood out as the strongest opponent of the new Constitution, arguing that sovereignty could

Above: *Eastern farmers poured into the West beginning in the eighteenth century. Tennessee, whose capital Nashville is shown here, became a state in 1796.*

Above: *James Monroe was governor of Virginia and a senator from his state before being elected president in 1816. His administration, the last of the long Virginia dynasty, was called the "Era of Good Feelings."*

not by nature be divided between state and nation, and he warned that a Northern-dominated Congress, loosely interpreting the Constitution, might some day emancipate the slaves during wartime – a remarkable prediction, even though he was thinking of a foreign war, not of the domestic conflict. Richard Henry Lee wrote an eloquent critique in his Letters of a Federal Farmer, but this was more than matched by Madison's ringing defense of the new document in the *Federalist Papers*. The South's defenses, he said, were adequate, and with its growing population, it would not be dominated. Insisting finally that there should be a bill of rights to protect both civil liberties and states' rights, Virginia ratified by a vote of 89 to 79.

George Washington, the first president of the United States under the new Constitution, was fifty-seven when he was inaugurated in 1789 and was one of the richest men in America. Though Washington professed to be above party, Southern sectionalism

was aggravated during his two administrations as he fell under the influence of Treasury Secretary Alexander Hamilton. The latter's program of economic nationalism – federal assumption of state debts, funding of the national debt at face value, passage of protective tariffs, creation of a national bank, federal support for manufacturing interests – brought about the creation of the first American system of political parties. The Federalists, who supported Hamilton's schemes, were pitted against the heavily Southern opposition, called the Republicans and led by Jefferson and Madison. Hamilton aimed to create national self-sufficiency resting on strong central government and a mixed economy, and his success depended on binding the commercial classes to the national state. His measures were thus designed to appeal, in the 1790s, to a relatively small group of people, and not necessarily to win the confidence of the ninety percent of the population who were farmers. While his program proved to be economically nationalistic and successful, it was psychologically divisive.

In 1793, Jefferson resigned his post as secretary of state in Washington's cabinet and, with Madison, formed a largely agrarian opposition to defend agricultural interests and states' rights against the centralizing tendencies of the new government. John Randolph of Roanoke, John Taylor of Caroline, James Monroe, Charles Pinckney, Nathaniel Macon, and John Breckinridge numbered among the party's leaders. Though Virginian in inception and always Southern in tone, the new party did broaden its base of support to include the rest of the country. The ideological division between it and the Federalists was sharper than was common in much of the subsequent history of American parties. The planters and farmers who were its members understood the good life and, to an extent, economics too, as seen through an agrarian lens. True wealth, they believed, sprang from the soil, and those who farmed that soil in harmony with God's natural laws formed society's most virtuous and stable element. Conversely, they despised cities and were wary of the dirty, downtrodden manufacturing classes who held no real property and thus no position in society. These first Republicans (there would later be another party of the same name but of utterly different provenance and purpose) believed in laissez-faire government. Their greatest fear sprang from a conviction that if commercial and manufacturing interests were joined to a strong central government, they would inevitably plunder the agricultural classes. The best government, they said, was the government that stayed closest to the people, and to ward off Hamilton's alarming program and protect the states, they insisted on strict interpretation of the Constitution.

George Washington was succeeded by John Adams of Massachusetts, the second and last Federalist president. His single term was marked by the growing strength of the opposition Republicans, by naval hostilities with France, and by passage of the Alien Act and the Sedition Act. Designed as partisan Federalist legislation to discourage criticism from the Republican press and to discourage immigrants from swelling the Republican ranks, the Alien Act and the Sedition Act triggered the first formal threat of secession from the Union. The Virginia and Kentucky resolves of 1798 – the Virginia Resolves were written by Madison, the Kentucky Resolves by Jefferson – set forth the compact theory of the Union and argued that when the states had voluntarily joined together to form the Union, they had specifically delegated certain powers to it but had reserved for themselves all powers not so delegated. A second set of resolutions asserted that in cases where disputes arose between the federal and state governments, the state had the right to judge whether an act of Congress might be enforced within its borders, which would, in effect, nullify violations by the federal government of the Constitution, as strictly construed. No other states responded favorably to the Resolves, and the crisis passed with the election of Thomas Jefferson to the presidency in 1800. But the principles that the Resolves set forth – that the Union was a compact among the sovereign states, which had entered into it freely and could therefore leave it freely – lay from the 1820s until the Civil War at the heart of the states' rights doctrine that the South pressed so vigorously into the defense of slavery.

The presidency of Thomas Jefferson ushered in the palmy days of the "Virginia dynasty": for the next twenty-five years Virginia planters would occupy the White House and would preside over a nation generally enjoying a flush of nationalism and optimism about its prospects. For its part, the South entered into the most nationalistic phase of its history.

Jefferson and his largely Southern-led Republican Party in some ways halted the trend toward centralization of governmental power, but they did not reverse it. Unable or unwilling to translate all of his agrarian principles into action, Jefferson dismantled some of Hamilton's programs, modified others, and left others as they stood. Now that he was in power and not merely the "loyal opposition," Jefferson showed two sides to his character. Jefferson "the good Republican" simplified the operations of government; he repealed the federal excise tax and let the Alien Act and the Sedition Act expire. He halted the expansion of the navy and reduced the standing army; he sped up repayment of the public debt; and he attacked Federalist appointments to the

judiciary. Indeed, he would have appointed a strict constructionist, Virginian Spencer Roane, to the Supreme Court, if the departing John Adams had not first named a nationalist, Virginian John Marshall.

Jefferson "the nationalist" would not turn out in practice to be quite the strict constructionist he had been in theory, and some of his Republican supporters railed at his betrayal of the principles on which he had been elected. In 1803, Jefferson bought the vast Louisiana Territory from Napoleon although there was nothing in the Constitution that gave the president the right to acquire new lands. He refused to abolish one chief agency of Hamilton's centralizing program, the Bank of the United States. In 1804, he approved a plan calling for a protective tariff, and he called for an amendment permitting the federal government to subsidize internal improvements, as public works – chiefly harbors, canals, and roads – were then called. In 1805, he asked Congress for money to buy Florida from Spain.

The difference was thus one of emphasis, not a fundamental change in philosophy, for Jefferson believed the republic was safe in the hands of the Republicans. John Randolph of Roanoke, an

Facing page: *Thomas Jefferson, Patrick Henry, F. L. Lee, and R. H. Lee draft the Declaration of Independence in this engraving entitled "In the Old Raleigh Tavern."*

Above left: *Henry Clay of Kentucky was an outstanding political leader in the 1820s. During that time, he developed his "American System," whereby the West would support the North on protective tariffs in return for the North's support on federal funding for canals and roads.*

Above: *Thomas Jefferson at his desk. Jefferson entered politics in 1769 as a member of the Virginia House of Burgesses. He served as governor of Virginia, minister to France, and secretary of state before being elected president in 1800.*

aristocratic slaveholder, long-time Jefferson supporter, and leader of the Republicans in the House of Representatives, did not agree and opposed the President on every apparent compromise of principle. Sometimes called the "Father of Southern Sectionalism," Randolph invoked states' rights and agrarian theory throughout both of Jefferson's administrations in order to defend the old republican order. All men were not created equal in either capacity or ability, and government attempts to make them so led to certain tyranny. "I love liberty; I hate equality," he put it plainly, and on his death, he freed his 400 slaves. John Taylor of Caroline, another Virginian, also broke with Jefferson over certain policies and emerged as the most consistent philosopher of agrarianism in the country. His closely reasoned, if turgid, treatises against the tariff, *Tyranny Unmasked*, and the Bank of the United States, *Construction Construed and Constitution Vindicated*, did more to assert states' rights than anything before John C. Calhoun's nullification arguments in the 1830s.

Such opponents within the Republican house (by the end of Jefferson's presidency they called themselves the "Old Republicans") neither split the party nor utterly derailed it, but they did keep alive the doctrines of sectionalism and states' rights during a period when the flood of nationalism in the South was otherwise at its peak. The administrations of Jefferson and his Virginian successors, James Madison and James Monroe, were so successful that the Federalist Party died after 1812, when, in the context of a second war with Britain, it was Federalist New England, and not the South, that seriously threatened disunion. Between 1815, which marked America's second and final victory over her old colonial master, and 1819, which brought severe economic depression, America experienced a heady mix of great prosperity and expansive nationalism, and Southerners partook of this fully. The young "War Hawks" of 1812 were Southerners from the Tidewater and the newer western regions – Kentucky's Henry Clay; South Carolina's John C. Calhoun (then very much the nationalist), William Lowndes, and Langdon Cheeves; Georgia's William Crawford; Tennessee's Felix Grundy. They all believed in a decisive "American destiny," which included expansion into the West and which was to be embodied in a deliberate program of economic nationalism. The program embraced a national banking system, tariffs to protect infant American industries, and federal support for internal improvements, and Henry Clay dubbed it "The American System." Enthusiasm for the program among Republicans, who had become the only remaining political party, demonstrated how far the Republicans had strayed from the pristine principles of the 1790s.

Above: *James Madison of Virginia was elected president in 1808. During his two-term administration, the War of 1812 brought to a conclusion, through the Treaty of Ghent, the conflict with England over navigation of the open seas .*

Above: *Thomas Jefferson reads a draft of the Declaration of Independence to Benjamin Franklin in this painting by Clyde O. de Land. The Declaration is regarded as America's fundamental political document.*

What brought this house if not quite down, then to the point of serious division, was the onset of hard times after the panic of 1819 and the dawning realization that the economic interests and probable patterns of future development of the North and the South were not only far from identical but were perhaps not even complementary. As the price of cotton tumbled seventy-five percent and the industrial revolution took hold in the North, old sectional realities, based since colonial times on subtle but profound cultural differences, re-emerged now heightened by economic grievances. When this was combined, from the 1830s, with the emergence of the slavery issue as the most powerful agent of sectionalism, one era in Southern history gave way to another. The nationalist South, which had won independence in concert with the North, written the Constitution, and forged the federal republic, gave way to the sectional South, which, due to the burden of slavery and its own understandings of the American polity and the good life, finally forsook that republic for a nation of its own imaginings.

3

THE ANTEBELLUM ERA

There is something about the history of the South between the Revolutionary War and the Civil War that makes it, in the popular imagination, loom larger and more vividly than any other moment. That period of time is strewn with durable images of masters and slaves and Southern belles, of plantation houses with white pillars and broad fields of cotton. This is the South immortalized in Margaret Mitchell's *Gone With the Wind* and trivialized in countless subsequent volumes of historical romance. It is a South that seems both content and sure of itself as being a place apart from, and superior to, the rest of America, even as it headed for disaster. It is a picture that only truly characterizes the South of the late antebellum period and then only unevenly, and it is a South that was the product of a gradual evolution.

To understand that point of arrival, it helps first to consider the texture of Southern life before the divisiveness of sectionalism took hold and then to observe the political flashpoints that marked the South's increasing self-awareness as a place apart, with a destiny all its own. On the eve of the antebellum era, the South was very much at peace with the rest of the nation. In the late 1810s, before the Missouri controversy ripped open the slavery question, there was no Southern political party, there was no slave bloc in Congress, and there was no sense of a purely Southern nationalism. The South had ample reason to be satisfied with national affairs. The Republican Party – then the only political party worthy of the name, and not to be confused with the antislavery party of Abraham Lincoln, which was not founded until the 1850s – was strongly influenced by Southerners. James Monroe, a Southerner and the last of the "Virginia dynasty," was still president; William Crawford of Georgia, John C. Calhoun of South Carolina, and William Wirt of Virginia constituted half of Monroe's cabinet. Henry Clay of Kentucky was speaker of the House of Representatives. The flush of nationalism from the Revolution itself and from the second war with

Left: the election of Andrew Jackson ushered in a period marked by the rise of the common man. Although Jackson himself purported to be just such a man, he was actually one of the richest men in Tennessee, with a fine plantation called The Hermitage, near Nashville. In this 1880 engraving, Jackson is shown greeting people in a small town during a stop on his way to Washington, D.C., following his election.

Below: *with his invention of the cotton gin in 1793, Eli Whitney helped change the face of the South. Adopted wherever greenseed cotton was grown, the machine sped the process of separating seeds from the cotton fibers. The large-scale production of cotton was now possible, and farmers and plantation owners in Georgia, Alabama, Mississippi, and West Tennessee made as much as $50 profit per acre.*

Britain in 1812 still warmed the land. Five signers of the Declaration of Independence were still alive. Thomas Jefferson, its author, was still master of his magnificent mountaintop house, Monticello, in Virginia, and was also still a reminder of the boldness of the American national experiment and of America's genius for a new kind of politics.

But if the South was politically still at peace with the rest of America, there were palpable differences in its cultural and economic life from which political particularism, aggravated by the debate over slavery and western expansion, would grow in time. At the time the Constitution was written, and for some years into the early history of the young republic, it appeared that the population of the Southern states would at least equal, and perhaps even exceed, that

of the North. But the census of 1820 revealed a disturbing fact: the population of the ten states south of Pennsylvania and the Ohio River – Maryland, Virginia, North and South Carolina, and Georgia, plus the younger western states of Kentucky, Tennessee, Alabama, Mississippi, and Louisiana – had declined as a proportion of the national whole to about 4.3 million, which was half a million short of half the national population.

As important, the character of this population was different from the population of the North. A third of it was black, and most of that was enslaved; in the North the figure for blacks was just two percent. There were about 116,000 free blacks in the South and about the same number in the North, but there were 1.5 million slaves in the South and

Below: *a cotton plantation on the Lower Mississippi River. After the War of 1812, when threat of attack by Native Americans was removed from the lower South, planters moved into the delta area of the Lower Mississippi and the "Black Belt" region of central Alabama and northern Mississippi. Wherever they moved, they brought with them a plantation system firmly tied to slavery and the production of cotton.*

practically none in the North. There were some 2.6 million white Southerners, but approximately twice that many white Northerners. Within the South, the white population was remarkably homogeneous, with only 12,000 unnaturalized foreigners, compared with more than 40,000 in the North. The colonial Southern melting pot of English, Irish, Scots, and Germans had done its job pretty well; obviously there was still some variation, but much less than in the North, whose cities would soon swell with new and ever greater waves of European immigration, little of which reached the South.

The absolute numbers in 1820 still mirrored the old colonial demographics. One in every four Southerners was a Virginian; not even one in twenty-five lived in Louisiana. Maryland, Virginia, and

North Carolina boasted half of the entire Southern population; the three southwestern states of Mississippi, Alabama, and Louisiana were home to less than one-tenth. But these were also the areas that were growing most quickly. Between 1810 and 1820, the white population of Tennessee, Alabama, Mississippi, and Louisiana increased by fifty percent, while that of Maryland, Virginia, and the Carolinas rose just twelve percent. There were also significant variations with regard to slavery. At one extreme, slaves constituted nearly fifty-three percent of the population of South Carolina and were also in the majority in Louisiana; in Tennessee they accounted for just nineteen percent of the total. But it was only in Tennessee and Kentucky that blacks accounted for less than one-third of the population.

Black or white, slave or freeman, the South's was a population clearly bound to agriculture and with few signs of movement into other areas of economic activity. All America was a farming country, with an average of seventy-seven percent of its citizens engaged in agriculture, but in the South that figure was ninety percent. And the quality of Southern agriculture differed from Northern, for in addition to feeding itself on its own corn, wheat, vegetables, hogs, cattle, and chickens, the South raised vast quantities of the great staple crops for sale on world markets. These crops – tobacco, rice, sugar, hemp, and particularly cotton – constituted the wealth of the region and had no equivalent outside the South. Back in the seventeenth century, tobacco was the crop that had made an economic success of the very first Southern colony, Virginia, and though it was hard on the soil, it proved a durable commodity in Virginia, North Carolina, and Kentucky, with 100 million pounds being exported in the early 1820s plus that raised for domestic consumption. Hemp was tobacco's rival in Kentucky, and though production was relatively small, it met the steady demand for bagging, rope, and baling material needed for cotton in the Lower South. Rice had once made South Carolina great, and its labor-intensive cultivation had brought massive numbers of slaves to the tidal swamplands. From only about 60,000 acres, 600 highly capitalized planters produced three-quarters of America's crop. Long-staple or sea-island cotton, which similarly required fertile land, heat, and humidity, was also hoed by the hordes of blacks who in the Carolina coastal region outnumbered whites by three to one. Sugar was the chief crop in Louisiana and required great investment in both land and slaves. Sugar was unique among Southern staple crops in its dependence on tariff protection.

But it was short-staple cotton that became the antebellum South's greatest crop, the one that could be grown all over the South either by gangs of slaves

Above: *a Currier & Ives lithograph of the Battle of Molino del Rey near Mexico City, on Setpember 8, 1847. General Zachary Taylor led the American troops against the Mexicans and within a week of the declaration of war had pushed the Mexican troops south of the Rio Grande.*

Left: *Eli Whitney began work on his cotton gin while visiting a plantation in Georgia. His gin made quick work of separating cotton fiber from seed, increasing productivity fiftyfold over the manual process.*

Facing page: *an illustrated front page dated September 2, 1839, of the abolitionist newspaper, Emancipator. The newspaper was one of many devoted to spreading the word of the anti-slavery movement.*

or by white yeomen, on rough land as well as fertile. By 1820, it had already surpassed all other Southern produce, and three-quarters of the crop of 353,000 bales went for export. Over the next thirty years, the price declined steadily, but yields increased, almost doubling in every decade up to the Civil War. It was a plant that would grow anywhere and so, like so much in nineteenth-century America, cotton moved west. In 1820, the Georgia and South Carolina Piedmont was the biggest producer, but by 1840 South Carolina had dropped to fifth place, and Mississippi sat at the top. By then more than half the crop came from west of the Atlantic seaboard states. For many, cotton represented their big chance, not just of making a living but of achieving real success, and the legendary path from dog-trot cabin to white-columned splendor was genuinely trodden by countless Southerners who started with little, but who, by the 1850s, took their proud place as grandees of "The Cotton Kingdom." Before the railroad era, which did not reach much of the South until the 1840s and 1850s, the need to transport bulky 500-pound bales of cotton to market put a premium on water transportation and briefly sustained the fleets of steamboats that plied the Mississippi River beginning in 1811.

However, it was not agricultural patterns alone that distinguished this early antebellum South from other places in America. In 1820, there were in the slave states just seven cities with more than 8,000 people, and Baltimore, which was the biggest at 62,000, sat on the very edge of the region. All of the others – New Orleans at 27,000, Charleston at 24,000, Washington, D.C. at 13,000, Richmond at 12,000, Norfolk and Alexandria at 8,000 apiece – were seaports (or in the case of Washington, a government center) engaged primarily in trade rather than manufacturing. Southern towns developed almost without exception along coasts or fall lines that separated the interior uplands from the coastal plains. At this moment there was no town of more than 2,500 inhabitants that was not on navigable water. Many of these places worked almost as city-states after the manner of colonial Charleston, though not nearly so opulent, with a river as their bond with the agricultural hinterland and the ocean as their corridor to the outside world, where the fruits of that hinterland found their market. But it was always decentralized, for Southern rivers diverged outward along an extensive coastline, which mitigated against the development of any single great metropolitan entrepot. Baltimore and New Orleans were on the edges, with ties as close to New York and Liverpool as to any Southern outback. The smaller towns scattered across the region were agricultural service centers, some of them becoming county seats and others becoming adorned in time with churches, schools, and colleges. In this they did not differ much from their Northern counterparts as centers of cultural, religious, and political life in an agricultural region, the rural gathering places for a farming people.

The South's increasing reliance on staple-crop agriculture had consequences both inside and outside the region that no one could fully foresee. Indeed then, with cotton constituting the lion's share of American exports, that reliance did not seem excessive. But Southerners relied heavily on others to transport their precious staples to faraway markets, as they themselves sailed few ships and built almost none. Thus, like it or not, they found themselves locked into a sort of triangular trade, in which cotton from the South went to England, manufactured goods from England and Europe came to New York City, and these were then sold to the South. It was a far-flung economic system, which in general relied on the factories of the Old World, the commercial and transportation services of the American Northeast, and the staple agricultural products of the American South. As a key player in such an international system, Southerners came early and strongly to believe in free trade as a cornerstone of their prosperity. Potential for abuse surely existed, but the pattern usually fitted the region's needs, and

EMANCIPATOR—EXTRA.

NEW-YORK, SEPTEMBER 2, 1839.

American Anti-Slavery Almanac for 1840.

The seven cuts following, are selected from thirteen, which may be found in the Anti-Slavery Almanac for 1840. They represent well-authenticated facts, and illustrate in various ways, the cruelties daily inflicted upon three millions of native born Americans, by their fellow-countrymen! A brief explanation follows each cut.

The peculiar "Domestic Institutions of our Southern brethren."

Selling a Mother from her Child.

Mothers with young Children at work in the field.

A Woman chained to a Girl, and a Man in irons at work in the field.

"They can't take care of themselves"; explained in an interesting article.

Hunting Slaves with dogs and guns. A Slave drowned by the dogs.

Servility of the Northern States in arresting and returning fugitive Slaves.

Southerners generally felt well served by it. With their exports exceeding $30 million a year, some Southerners enjoyed great credit far and wide and displayed it splendidly. Greenwood Leflore, a Choctaw Indian and highly successful planter with more than 400 slaves, spent some $10,000 in France on the furnishings for a single room in his Mississippi plantation house; these included oriental rugs, tortoise-shell cabinet work, and Louis XIV chairs and sofas.

Insofar as Southerners manufactured things for themselves, they made relatively simple items needed to service the needs of their agricultural society: they worked with wood, iron, and hides, and they ground grain into meal, grits, and flour. In most of the South, the white artisan class, which also had to compete with trained plantation and urban slaves, were too few in number and too dependent on agriculture to become as important as they would be in the North. Such trades were all very small-time, with usually only two or three men to a shop, and they served largely local markets. By contrast, tobacco and iron were sometimes worked in establishments of considerable size. Virginia, which was the nation's largest coal producer, turned out pig iron, castings, nails, firearms, and farm implements. In both Virginia and Kentucky, tobacco factories transformed half the tobacco crop into plugs and twists for chewing and into snuff, pipe tobacco, and cigars.

The distribution of even such modest manufacturing resulted in the greatest concentration of factories in Virginia, Maryland, and Kentucky, which contained the larger establishments and two-thirds of all those Southerners who in 1820 did not make their living from the land. Sugar mills were limited to Louisiana, rice mills to South Carolina, and cotton gins were everywhere, but all of these activities were closely and necessarily attached to the equipment and activities of the farms and plantations. And even though the Upper South contained more factories than any other place in the South, it was still hardly enough to count: there were probably more field hands in some single counties of the South Carolina Low Country in 1820 than there were factory workers in the whole South.

It would be a mistake however to regard the South, at this point still forty years before the Civil War, as a place powerfully united by either character or conviction. Two types of internal tension in particular strained the unity of Southern life and had political ramifications as the antebellum years wore on. The conflict between Low Country and Up Country reached back to colonial times, when the coastal regions of South Carolina and Virginia had boasted more advanced social institutions, more ample material possessions (including more slaves),

Above: *a hero of the War of 1812, Andrew Jackson was a popular president whose two terms marked a movement towards greater political democracy in the United States.*

Right: *the antebellum South was not a place unified by a single character. There was much conflict between the eastern regions and the western areas and between the Upper and Lower South.*

and larger towns than the remoter regions. In Tennessee, it was the fertile central and western regions that corresponded to "Low Country," while the mountainous eastern sections played the role of "the backwoods." In Mississippi, "Low Country" meant Natchez and the southwestern corner of the state, while the poorer frontier region lay up in the northeast. Obviously much could depend on which of these groups controlled the state governments, and the unity of the South would depend in part on whether the same type of groups were in power in each of the Southern states.

The second source of internal division was between the upper South and the cotton, or deep, South. Agriculture in Virginia, Maryland, and Kentucky was more diversified, and much of those states' produce was sold domestically; they boasted more commerce and manufacturing and enjoyed greater proximity to the outside world. In most of

Below: *Greenwood Plantation near St. Francisville, Louisiana. Built in 1830 by Ruffin Barrow, this palatial mansion tells of the great wealth enjoyed by plantation owners in the antebellum era of the nineteenth century.*

the deep South, cotton was the predominant money crop, with rice and sugar at the edges, and it sold abroad on the world market. The upper South had more free blacks; the deep South had the heaviest concentration of slaves. Of all the Southern states, South Carolina probably shared the least with anybody else. Virginia still enjoyed the most revered heritage but seemed somehow to be losing its economic and political grip. And the transmontane states such as Tennessee and Mississippi were

assuming new vigor and importance every year, just as their counterparts, Ohio and Indiana, were in the old Northwest.

The catastrophe and ruin that came at the end of the antebellum period, while hardly inevitable, had their seeds in certain unfinished business left over from the founding of the Republic. When the American colonies first broke from Britain, then experimented with the Articles of Confederation, and finally forged a bold new constitution on which

Below right: *slaves being readied for boarding a ship to America. By 1750, more than 200,000 slaves lived in colonial America, and over the next fifty years a million more were imported.*

to build their new nation in the wilderness, everyone knew that one of the large problems that had to be solved was how to reconcile the interests of diverse geographical sections with the necessity of national unity. The principle of federalism as it was embodied in the Constitution of 1787 provided the chief means to this end. By dividing sovereignty between the newly formed federal government and the existing state governments, the founders hoped to preserve local liberties and to establish a national state powerful enough to survive in an unfriendly world. Sectionalism obviously antedated the new constitutional arrangements, and it would characterize life in the United States for decades to come. Even colonial America was a very large place in which North and South especially, by the time of the Revolution, had already developed distinct cultures and outlooks. The founders knew this well, coming themselves from both Northern and Southern colonies, but they saw no fatal danger in it as long as one section more or less balanced the other, and as long as, in a majoritarian system of government, the rights of the minority could be protected.

The South, characterized as it was by staple-crop agriculture that was tied to world markets and made possible with the help of slavery, proved to be the most durable of the sections, and, as time passed, the one whose interests seemed to diverge most from the nation's as a whole. In the eighteenth century, the South's great crops had been the crops of seaboard Virginia and South Carolina: tobacco and rice. In the nineteenth century, it was short-staple cotton, which would grow anywhere. The introduction of Eli Whitney's cotton gin made possible the rapid combing of the short-staple plant and thus vastly increased the South's cotton output and its profitability. Slavery,

which had attached itself firmly to the South in colonial times, proved well adapted to the cotton trade and helped fuel its expansion.

Much of the enlightened opinion of the age, both in the North and the South, had doubts about the morality of the institution. In the 1770s, Thomas Jefferson, author of the Declaration of Independence and a slaveholder until the day he died, proposed repatriating – "colonizing" as it came to be known – the blacks back to Africa. In the early years of the new century, this idea, which reflected Southerners' guilt about the institution itself and their fear of the blacks in their midst, gained a wide following in the South. It was obviously a Southern problem and one that involved both the moral problem of holding other humans in perpetual bondage and the practical problem of what to do with an alien race should it be emancipated. The American Colonization Society was founded in 1816 and was headed by Southerners James Madison, James Monroe, and John Marshall from Virginia and supported by Henry Clay from Kentucky. Of the 143 emancipation societies in existence in the country in 1826, 103 had been founded in the South, many of them by Quaker Benjamin Lundy, who spread the abolition message through the mountainous regions of Tennessee and North Carolina. In addition, there were in the South several anti-slavery newspapers, including the *Emancipator* in Tennessee, the *Abolition Intelligencer* in Kentucky, and the *Genius of Universal Emancipation* in Baltimore.

It was not a modern, color-blind morality that moved these men, but an eighteenth-century rationalist one that was also combined with a profound racialism. If the slaves should be freed, then the freedmen must also be removed from the area. Means other than slavery of controlling masses

N. B. FOREST,
DEALER IN SLAVES,
No. 87 Adams-st, Memphis, Ten.,

HAS just received from North Carolina, twenty-five likely young negroes, to which he desires to call the attention of purchasers. He will be in the regular receipt of negroes from North and South Carolina every month. His Negro Depot is one of the most complete and commodious establishments of the kind in the Southern country, and his regulations exact and systematic, cleanliness, neatness and comfort being strictly observed and enforced. His aim is to furnish to customers A. 1 servants and field hands, sound and perfect in body and mind. Negroes taken on commission.   jan21

of blacks were not then generally considered, and the idea of equality was utterly unthinkable. Some blacks were in fact "colonized" back to Africa, and the west African nation of Liberia owes its existence to the movement; its capital city, Monrovia, was actually named for President James Monroe. But the numbers were simply too daunting – and the economic stakes simply too high – for colonization ever to be tried widely. Besides, there was the pull of cotton, which was so compatible with slavery, and which not only profited the Southern planters but also represented the bulk of United States exports and fueled the entire national economy. For a young country trying to establish itself, Southern cotton, whether or not it was grown by slaves, constituted a tremendous economic resource that no one was prepared to put at risk.

With colonization providing an outlet for moral frustrations about slavery, and with cotton constituting a key to national prosperity, it would seem that the matter of slavery might not necessarily have led, as it did, to the dissolution of the Union and civil war. Indeed, slavery, although "built-in" to the "three-fifths" clause of the Constitution, was otherwise left as something to be regulated by the several states as they themselves saw fit. So it might have remained, at least for a much longer time, had the new American nation been a fixed, static place, as most older nations were by then. But America in

Above: *an advertisment for slaves in a Memphis newspaper in the 1850s. The abolition movement was not strictly a Northern cause in the 1830s. By 1826, 103 emancipation societies had been founded in the South.*

Right: *a slave auction in Charleston, South Carolina. Southerners who favored emancipation usually also favored colonization – the relocation of freed blacks to Africa.*

the early nineteenth century was a land on the verge of both economic growth and geographical expansion the likes of which the world had not seen before, and it is in this context that slavery – localized in the South but linked to the growth of the cotton trade – became the explosive issue of the later antebellum era. The world had seen nations undergo great territorial expansion before, usually advancing by imperial means and then resorting to unitary rule from older established centers of power. But what was about to happen in America was different and, in the long run, would prove to have been a great strength first in forging, and then in holding together, a diverse and continental nation. In the short run however, it invited the resurgence of sectionalism, which increasingly meant the slavery question, and finally provoked the constitutional crisis that nearly ended the American experiment.

Thomas Jefferson called it forging "an empire for liberty": the process of state-making outlined in the

Northwest Ordinance of 1787 which became the manual for the orderly growth of the American republic westward across the continent. At the time of the Revolution, the fledgling nation comprised merely thirteen seaboard colonies strung out from Maine to Georgia and backed against a vast continent to which they had no title and seemed unlikely to obtain it. In the late eighteenth and early nineteenth centuries, Americans had gradually crested the Appalachian Mountains and had begun to settle the interior of the Ohio Valley; the states of the Old Northwest and the Old Southwest were the result. But when, in 1803, Thomas Jefferson acquired the entire Louisiana Territory, which reached from the Mississippi River to the crest of the Rocky Mountains, from a panicky Napoleon, and when, in the 1840s, pushy expansionists picked a fight with Mexico, secured California and the Southwest, and reached the edge of the western ocean, America found itself to be a continental nation. From this vast territory would be carved a score of new states – not colonies – and, after a territorial apprenticeship, each would be admitted to the Union on the basis of full equality with the older eastern commonwealths. So it was that North Dakota and New Mexico would each send two senators to Washington, just as New York and Virginia did, while their populations would determine their level of representation in the House of Representatives.

The letter of that process was written down. It had already been applied and shown to work with the admission of trans-Appalachian states such as Ohio and Tennessee. The trouble arose with regard to the spirit of the process and the open-ended question of what sort of society should be fitted into the clever constitutional framework of new sovereign states within a sovereign union. It was in this context that slavery ceased to be merely a local Southern matter, and that Southern sectionalism, which was increasingly aggravated by both anti- and pro-slavery arguments, pushed the nation toward disunion. These were not theoretical questions, and as the 1820s began, Americans in both North and South got a sudden glimpse of just how volatile the mixture of slavery and western expansion could be.

In 1819 there were twenty-two states, eleven slave and eleven free – the careful result of admitting first one type and then the other so as to maintain

Left: a slave market in Atlanta, Georgia. Most white Southerners worked their farms without slave labor, or with only one or two field hands. Good farm hands cost as much as $1,500 by the 1850s, far more than the average farmer could afford. Only in the deep South, where huge cotton plantations spread across the landscape, was there a great concentration of slaves.

equal representation in the Senate. The problem came in the House where, even with the advantage of the three-fifths clause, the slave states, falling behind their Northern sisters, filled eighty-one seats compared with the North's 105. At this early stage, it is foolish to dwell too closely on purely sectional divisions in the halls of the national government. The only political party worthy of the name, the Republicans, was a national organization with major constituents, united by class and interest, on both sides of the Mason-Dixon Line. The same would be true of the Whig Party as it developed in the 1830s and 1840s. It was the Whigs' purpose not to exacerbate but to soothe sectional antagonisms, which they managed to do reasonably well until the last decade before the Civil War. But, in 1820, what focused attention so sharply on the matter of Congressional balance was the imminent admission to the Union of Missouri. It was an occasion with precedent-setting potential; if Missouri went "free," Southerners had reason to fear that so might the whole of the trans-Mississippi West. If that happened, the South, with its "peculiar institution" and hordes of black slaves, would find itself in a permanent minority in the national government. Should that government then ever chose to amend the Constitution so as to attack slavery, the South would be at its mercy.

The enabling bill for the admission of Missouri, a territory settled largely by Southerners and where there were already some slaves, was introduced in the House of Representatives on March 16, 1818. Congress did not act on the bill during that session or the next. When the bill was next considered in February 1819, it came with an amendment attached from a New York congressman proposing that no more slaves should be introduced into the state and that those slaves already there should be emancipated at the age of twenty-five. Meanwhile, the Territory of Arkansas, situated just to the south of Missouri and whose northern border fell along the latitude of 36 degrees 30 minutes north, was organized by the Congress without restriction on slavery. The debate on Missouri was as contentious as it was fruitless. Representatives of free states based their arguments on the moral position that slavery was wrong. Southern representatives declared that the morality issue was irrelevant to the debate. In their view, Congress had no right to exclude slavery – whether moral or immoral – from a state. Here the debate was between those who interpreted the constitution loosely and proposed an extension of national power and those who interpreted the constitution strictly and were determined to preserve states' rights. In the political maneuverings in Congress, the states of the old Northwest Territory realigned themselves. Previously those states had voted in Congress as a

An invoice of ten negroes sent this day to John B Williamson by Geo Kremer named & cost as folras

To wit .. Betsey Kackley . . . . . . $ 410.00
Nancy Aulick 515.00
Harry & Helen Miller . . 1200.00
Mary Kootz 600.00
Betsey Ott 560.00
Isaac & Fanny Brent . . 992.00
Lucinda Luckett 467.50
George Smith 510.00

Amount of my traveling expences & boarding 5254.50
of lot No 9 not included in the other bills " 39.50
Kremers expences transporting lot No 9 to Rich 51.00
Carryall hire 6.00
$ 5351.00

I have this day delivered the above named negroes costing includeing my expences and other expences five thousand three hundred & fifty dollars this May 26th 1835

John W Pittman

I did intend to leave Nancy child but she made such a damned fuss I had to let her take it I could of got fifty Dollars for so you must add forty Dollars to the above

Above: *a bill of sale for ten black slaves. The total cost including the trader's expenses was $5,351. As the cost of slaves rose and opposition to slavery became* more vocal in the North, Southerners grew more committed to the institution. Some Southern states made it impossible for owners to free their slaves.

Right: *The Hermitage, near Nashville, Tennessee, was the home of President Andrew Jackson. Jackson moved to Tennessee at the age of nineteen and began acquiring* vast land holdings. At that time, Tennessee was more "Western" than "Southern" in character, and Jackson himself epitomized the new Western policial leaders.

bloc with the Southern states, believing there was a closer kinship with that region due to its agricultural character. With the debate over Missouri, however, the Ohio Valley states swung to the North. Southern congressmen began to suspect Northern motives. Doubting that their counterparts above the Mason-Dixon Line had the condition of slaves at heart, the Southern representatives feared that the debate had been engineered to gain domination over the South; political power, not morality, motivated the North Congressmen.

At last, on March 3, 1820, a final compromise was reached. Missouri would be admitted as a slave state but was to be paired with the admission of Maine as a free state. That much seemed fair to everyone and portended no ill for the future admission of other states. What did set off the alarm bells – though nothing could be done about it at the time – and what did set a new precedent was Congress's extension of the 36/30 latitude straight west across the whole Louisiana Purchase, for the purpose of clearly dividing future free from future slave territory. On the surface and in retrospect, this would seem a plausible enough thing to have done, but that is not

to take into account the expansive spirit of nationalism that was then suffusing American life and whose compelling symbol was the Great West. Congress, now boldly legislating with regard to slavery in the new territories acquired in the West since the Revolution, banned it from some of that territory not yet even organized into states. The 36/30 line cut across the boundless spirit of the age and left a livid scar that said the West was now divided. Thomas Jefferson most memorably captured the long-range meaning of what had happened. The Compromise struck him, he said, as a fire bell in the night, and he warned the nation that any such fixed geographical line that divided the North and the South and was identified with political and moral principles – in this case the issue of slavery – could never be erased peacefully. In the Compromise, the old Southern nationalist heard a distant death knell for the Union.

The Missouri Compromise had temporarily settled the question of slavery in the West by drawing a line across the territory. But the South's marriage to both staple-crop agriculture and the system of slave labor that made this possible continued to set the region apart from the rest of the country, even as

Above: *an engraving of Andrew Jackson's home, The Hermitage, near Nashville, Tennessee. The Ladies' Hermitage Association was founded in 1889 to help raise funds for the site's preservation. Today the home is operated as a historic house museum and attracts thousands of visitors annually.*

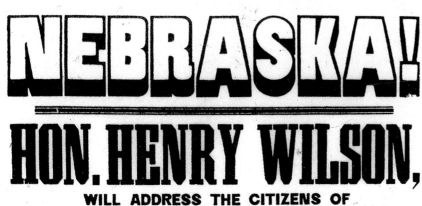

NEBRASKA!

HON. HENRY WILSON,

WILL ADDRESS THE CITIZENS OF

ASHBURNHAM,

—AT THE—

TOWN HALL,

On THURSDAY EVENING, March 23d,

AT SEVEN O'CLOCK,

ON THE SUBJECT OF THE

Nebraska Bill,

NOW BEFORE THE U. S. CONGRESS.

CITIZENS ALL, WHO FEEL AN INTEREST IN THE QUESTION OF

FREEDOM OR SLAVERY,

ARE EARNESTLY INVITED TO ATTEND.

PER ORDER OF THE COMMITTEE.

ASHBURNHAM, MARCH 18, 1854.

Garfield, Printer, Fitchburg

Above: a broadside announcing a public meeting in Ashburton to discuss the Nebraska Bill. The bill called for the establishing of two territories, Kansas and Nebraska, and leaving to the residents of the territories the decision on whether they would be slave or free states. The popular sovereignty called for by the bill did not comply with the provisions of the Missouri Compromise, a bill that prohibited the extension of slavery north of latitude 36° 30'.

cotton became an ever more valuable national asset. Cotton's value was tied to conditions in the world market, and the more the trade expanded and prospered, the more Southern agricultural interests became convinced that everything depended on free trade. So it was that, at the end of the 1820s, the issue of the tariff became as sectionally divisive as the issue of slavery expansion had been at their beginning.

The problem for a staple-crop producer such as the South was a classic dilemma of selling cheap, if the world price happened to be low, and buying dear, for the manufactured goods that Southern planters had to buy came at prices that were artificially inflated by tariff protection. As far as New England and Northeastern factory owners faced with competition from the frequently cheaper and superior goods of Europe's established manufacturers were concerned, protective duties encouraged growth in the early take-off stages of industrialization, and

protectionism remained a temptation throughout the nineteenth century – long after American industry was off and running.

Immediately after the Missouri debate had come to an end, Henry Baldwin, a representative from Pennsylvania, introduced a new tariff bill. Designed to provide revenue to the federal government and to protect manufacturing to a degree higher than the tariff of 1816, the bill proposed increases of from 20 to 100 percent on textiles, forged iron bars, glass, hemp, and other items. Baldwin and Henry Clay of Kentucky, Speaker of the House, explained that the tariff would aid more than just manufacturing concerns. Farmers – at least those who grew wheat, corn, and livestock – would benefit because with the increased prosperity of manufacturers would come improved markets for the farmers' produce. Opponents of the new tariff believed that manufacturing ought not to receive special protection. If left alone, the economy would eventually improve. At best, the tariff offered only a temporary cure to the economic slump.

When the measure came to a vote, it passed in the House 91 to 83. Southern states solidly opposed the bill, Middle Atlantic and Northwest states favored it and New England states, where shipping concerns nearly matched industrial ones, were almost evenly split. Voting along the same geographical lines, the Senate defeated the measure 22 to 21.

But the debate over tariffs was far from over. In 1823, reapportionment brought nineteen new seats to the Middle Atlantic and Ohio Valley states and nine new seats to the Southwestern states. The South Atlantic states received no new seats. On January 9, 1824, a new tariff bill was introduced, and for the next three months it was hotly debated. The protectionists had the votes they needed in the House, and the bill passed on April 16. In the Senate, Missouri's Senators swung to the side of protection, and the measure became law.

Throughout the 1820s, the tariff crept upward, and under Nationalist President John Quincy Adams it reached extremely protectionist levels following the law enacted in 1828. South Carolinian John C. Calhoun feared that unless the South could achieve relief, the Union would be disrupted, and that same year he anonymously authored the *South Carolina Exposition and Protest*, which expounded the doctrine of nullification and established Calhoun as the leading Southern sectionalist.

The man Southerners had hoped would save them, however, was another of their own: Andrew Jackson from Tennessee. His name identified the rising political persuasion of the age, Jacksonian Democracy, which stood for broader political participation, downward social leveling, the spoils system, and a shift in the political center of gravity from the old Tidewater to the booming states across the mountains.

Jackson relied not on his cabinet but on an informal group of friends for advice during his presidency. One reason Jackson turned away from his official cabinet and relied instead on his "Kitchen Cabinet" was his anger over the official cabinet's treatment of Peggy Eaton. Married first to a sailor, Peggy was the daughter of an innkeeper in Washington, D.C., where Jackson and John H. Eaton, a member of his official cabinet, often stayed. Rumors that Eaton was overly attentive toward Peggy while her husband was at sea flew about the District. When her husband died, more rumors circulated that he had killed himself after learning of his wife's affair. To stop the rumors, Eaton married Peggy, but she was never received with grace by Jackson's cabinet members and their wives.

Jackson was infuriated over what he considered a lack of manners in his Cabinet. His anger was stirred in part by the memory of the rumors that surrounded him and his wife Rachel. Jackson had married Rachel before her divorce from her first husband was final, and during his campaign for the presidency, the rumors became a hotly debated issue. Rachel died a month after he was elected, and he always believed that the muckraking nature of the campaign had brought her an early death. In the Cabinet, only Martin Van Buren showed any kindness to the Eatons, and Jackson came to feel that it was Vice-President John Calhoun and his wife who were their primary persecutors.

For his part, Calhoun became disenchanted with the President as well. As the tariff crisis built up and tempers shortened, Calhoun discovered that Jackson, the old military hero of the Battle of New Orleans in the War of 1812, was no half-hearted nationalist. The widening gap between the two men was demonstrated in 1830 at a dinner held on the anniversary of Thomas Jefferson's birth. Jackson offered his vice-president a toast provocative enough in the context of the moment: "Our Union. It must be preserved." Calhoun, surprised but quick on his feet, returned: "The Union. Next to liberty, most dear." Two years later, when yet another protective tariff was passed and signed into law by Jackson, Calhoun resigned as Vice-President and set out to make what seemed as if it might be the final defense

Right: *Captain May's charge at Resaca de la Palma. The Mexican War lasted a little less than two years. The Treaty of Guadalupe Hidalgo established the Rio Grande as the border between the United States and Mexico and transferred to the United States ownership of New Mexico and Upper California.*

Above: *William L. Yancey (1814-1863), a renowned orator and congressman, promoted the South's secession from the Union. The owner of a few influential Southern newspapers, Yancey worked tirelessly in the cause of states' rights.*

put upon by national policies and had in response threatened secession at the Hartford Convention. That awkward moment had quickly passed, and the sectional rift laid open by the tariff controversy of the early 1830s might also have faded to nothing if the Republic's western edge had still lain at the Mississippi River. But it already reached to the Rockies across a vast unorganized territory where the urgent task of building up a new society from nothing would not leave old sectional rivalries undisturbed. Even as the tariff declined as a divisive issue, that of slavery, which was infinitely more complex and emotional, took its place. And as the threats to slavery seemed to multiply, once moderate Southerners again raised radical doubts about the wisdom of union.

For a time, however, postponing the final settlement of these things seemed to work. Despite the Panic of 1837 and the national depression that followed, the faith of Americans, Southerners included, stayed strong through the 1830s and 1840s, and the country seemed safely launched on its united way. Immigrants swelled the Northern cities in which America's first industrial revolution took off decisively. Railroads crested the Appalachian Mountains and began to tie together the East and the West. In the South, even as some older seaboard regions languished, cotton proved to be king and expanded westward across Alabama and Mississippi into Arkansas and Texas. With this expansion went ambitious white men and troops of enslaved black ones. From thousands of farms and plantations newly carved from virgin wilderness came ever greater quantities of "The Great White Staple," destined for the textile mills of Europe and the North. But none of this was without an undertone of foreboding. Even if there had been no tariff controversy and no nullification crisis, other events would have served notice on attentive citizens that the moral contradictions presented by the existence of slavery in a land founded on principles of liberty would not leave the national conscience alone.

In 1831, just before the nullification crisis, when emancipation sentiment was still strong and respectable in the South, the legislature of the state of Virginia – the oldest part of the South and the place where blacks had first been introduced into America in 1619 – held wide-ranging debates on the question of emancipation. Many of the most respected leaders in the region still held that slavery was at best a necessary evil, and some famous leaders – George Washington, Robert Carter, and John Randolph – had actually freed their slaves in their wills; bankruptcy had prevented Thomas Jefferson from doing the same. The main sentiment behind the debates was anti-slavery, but it was also anti-

which meant that in matters of dispute between state and nation a majority of the people within a sovereign state would have to concur with the national legislature. His answer was not the one that was ultimately accepted, though it took a civil war to lay it to rest. His argument, that the union was composed of a compact of sovereign states and that those states must be supreme, was however the same argument that would be used thirty years later once the rest of the South was ready to come along.

As the nation expanded to the west and as the North's growth and vigor began clearly to outdistance the South's, support would grow for the final step in Calhoun's theory: secession from the Union. Reconciling minority rights with majoritarian rule was felt to be a problem by whoever happened to be in the minority, and during the War of 1812, it had been New England which had felt itself to be most

Above: *in October 1859, John Brown, a leader in the Pottawatomie Massacre in Kansas, struck again, this time in Harpers Ferry, Virginia. Backed by Northern abolitionists, the radical leader attempted to incite a slave rebellion and took over the arsenal. Federal troops captured Brown after a two-day siege.*

black, and what the Virginians were considering was not just the abstract question of the justice of emancipation, but the costs of compensating the owners and of transporting the freed blacks out of the country. Although these costs were deemed too high, emancipation under any other circumstances was deemed too great a threat to the peace and welfare of the state, and the Virginians finally rejected the emancipation alternative by a small majority. Because it occurred in Virginia, the oldest, most moderate, and most prestigious state in the South, the vote marked a turning point for the whole South. For nowhere else could a more thoughtful and enlightened debate be expected to take place.

The Virginia debate had taken place in the wake of two other events that deeply disturbed Southerners and served notice on them that they faced a perilous future. A fanatical black lay preacher named Nat Turner incited a slave revolt in Southampton County, Virginia, which resulted in sixty murders, mostly of white women and children. The rampage began before dawn on August 22, 1831, at the home of Turner's master, Joseph Travis. After killing the entire Travis family, Turner and his band swept across the county, from plantation to plantation, killing every white person they encountered. Gathering forces along the way – estimated variously at forty to two hundred – the band continued its deadly forays until the next morning. Then a party of white men scattered Turner's rebels and military troops joined the hunt, during which both innocent and guilty blacks were tortured and killed. Organized slave revolts had been rare in America, and Turner's rampage failed utterly to incite the large surrounding black population to a general rising; Turner and about fifty other blacks were promptly caught; twenty

were convicted and hanged. But coming when it did, the rebellion not only sent a chill down the spines of whites who lived in a lightly policed society amid thousands of enslaved blacks but also alerted them doubly to another, related danger from afar.

On January 1, 1831, in Boston, William Lloyd Garrison published the first issue of his radical abolitionist newspaper, The *Liberator*, and with it began the most sweeping moral crusade in American history. Garrison's influence extended far beyond the literal reach of his newspaper, which never had more than 3,000 subscribers. His intemperate style of denouncing all slaveholders as criminals and any law – including the United States Constitution – that defended slavery as "an agreement with hell" attracted the attention of moral crusaders and moderate men alike. In the North, which he chastised bitterly for its apathy toward the evils of slavery, Garrison probably had more enemies than friends – enemies who understood the sectional dangers of abolitionism. But what Garrison voiced so radically, a wide spectrum of respectable Northern opinion

generally agreed with. Slavery seemed ever more philosophically inconsistent with fundamental American principles, particularly as those principles were being elaborated every year as the nation welcomed immigrants from abroad and expanded westward. Moderate "free-soilers," while reluctant to meddle with slavery where it already existed, would restrict its growth in the Western territories. Philosophical abolitionists, such as Ralph Waldo Emerson and James Russell Lowell, believed slavery was evil at heart, as had many of the Founding Fathers, and anti-slavery leaders, such as Theodore Weld and Charles G. Finney, began to mobilize opinion that Garrison alone could never command, with the goal of somehow bringing slavery in America to an end. This was a time of reformism and evangelical religion, whose churches in the 1830s and 1840s reflected strong anti-slavery views. Some 2,000 abolitionist societies had sprung up by 1840; although local affairs they were a measure of a growing Northern consensus. In the emotionally charged atmosphere that the subject generated, appeal

Above left: *John Brown's notoriety came with his role in the Pottawatomie Massacre in Kansas in 1855. Accompanied by six free-soilers, Brown slipped into the pro-slavery settlement and killed five settlers. Fighting then spread throughout the territory, dubbed by the press "Bleeding Kansas."*

Above right: *Robert Tombs was a U.S. Representative from Georgia before the South seceded from the Union. He was one of the few ardent secessionists included in Jefferson Davis's cabinet, where he served as secretary of state.*

Above: *Richmond, Virginia, in the 1850s. Although the South remained firmly tied to agriculture, small manufactures did exist. In Virginia, the manufacture of chewing tobacco flourished, and by 1825 a cotton textile mill was thriving in Fayetteville, North Carolina. Industrialization spread slowly, however, and by 1860 only ten percent of the nation's manufactured goods were produced in the South.*

was increasingly made to the "higher law" that said all men are brothers in the sight of God and that was implicit in the very founding of America. Before such a "higher law," earthly laws that contradicted it could have no claim.

The story of the anti-slavery and the abolitionist crusade fills volumes, and is a subject that stands on its own even outside the history of the South. But as regards that history, there are two chief points to be made. The first is that the problem – slavery – that was coming so to agitate Northern opinion was a problem that was localized in the South. This meant that the link was easily made between "anti-slavery" and "anti-Southern." And in a loosely knit federal union any such agitation could be dangerous. Reformers in the North were casting the stone simultaneously at their own house – the United States – and at somebody else's – the South. To the very large extent that no Northerner was being asked to bear the burden of emancipation, it seemed to many Southerners that the North's allegedly noble convictions about the universal rights of man were

actually very cheap convictions to hold. Like no other issue before it, then, anti-slavery laid bare the critical sectional rifts inherent in the young American nation, even as that nation was striving to reproduce itself in the West. To oppose slavery was, to Southerners, to oppose the way the South lived and prospered; it was also to threaten the security of life and home, as the Nat Turner Rebellion had supposedly shown.

In addition, to some Northerners and self-interested Southerners, to oppose slavery was to oppose the fundamental constitutional compromise that had effectively brought the nation into being and to threaten the federal nature of the Union. For slavery, in the three-fifths clause, was part of the Constitution – a necessarily evil part in the opinion of the Founding Fathers perhaps, but a part nevertheless. And a part it remained for a later generation of Southerners who came to argue that slavery was in fact a positive good. The ever more frequent reference by Northern anti-slavery voices to a "higher law" – higher certainly than any Southern

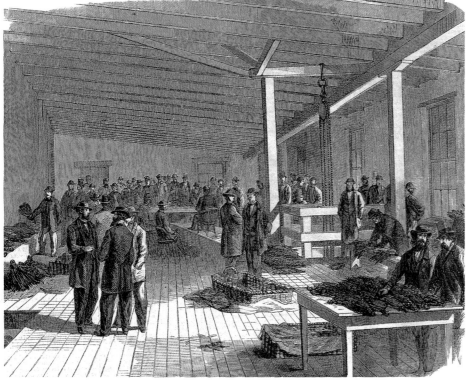

Top: *a view of Nashville, Tennessee, in the mid-nineteenth century. A contemporary description announced that the city had a population of 10,000 in 1840. It was further described as being home to ten churches, a "lunatic" asylum, a lyceum, and Nashville University,* *founded in 1806. The university had four professors and about a hundred students. After World War II, Nashville changed to a metropolitan government system to help deal with finances and suburbanization.*

Above: *the Tobacco Exchange in Richmond, Virginia. While tobacco remained an important crop in Virginia, by 1849 the state's wheat crop was worth more than twice as much as the tobacco grown there.*

slave code, but also higher than the Constitution itself – brought the true Union-shattering potential of the slavery issue to the forefront of American life.

In a sense, either side could claim that it was the other side that threatened the Union. Northern anti-slavery voices argued that no nation founded on liberty could live up to those first principles as long as it tolerated slavery anywhere in its midst. Southern pro-slavery voices argued that when the Union was put together in the 1780s, it was done in the full knowledge of the existence of slavery in the Southern states, whose concern and whose concern alone slavery must remain. To attack slavery, therefore, was to attack the compact that had been made between the states that constituted the Union; it was to put something else – a "higher law" – above the Union. This was, of course, exactly what Northerners would accuse Southerners of when the latter spoke of nullification and the right of a State to secede: of putting something else – States' rights – above the Union. It all depended on where a man stood, and from the 1830s, Southerners stood more and more on defensive ground.

As the anti-slavery movement and the abolitionists shouted about a "higher law," the South responded with a defense of slavery as a positive good and erected an elaborate structure of economic, ethnological, and Biblical arguments defending it. Thomas R. Dew, James H. Hammond, William Gilmore Simms, James D. B. De Bow, George Fitzhugh, Edmund Ruffin, and, of course, John C. Calhoun led a throng of voices that warned of abolition's dire consequences: economic ruin for the South and the nation, destitution for the blacks, and extermination for the whites. They argued that the Old and the New Testaments were strewn with references to masters and servants. Paul had commanded obedience, and Christ himself had never spoken against the institution, which was all around him. Slavery had obviously worked well for the Greeks and Romans, so much of whose civilizations nineteenth-century Americans professed to admire. Immutable laws of nature, pro-slavery apologists argued, ordained a "mudsill class," on whose crude labors a higher culture could be built by those of superior knowledge and power. In the South, so the argument went, this meant a cultured and leisured white planter class at the top and, at the bottom, black slaves whose natural burden it was to hew the wood and haul the water, but whose inestimable benefit it also was to have been redeemed from African savagery and converted to Christianity. The slaves suffered no greater physical hardships than did Northern "wage slaves," and they enjoyed a good bit more security.

The result was a South that, in defense against a

pitiless abolitionist onslaught, convinced itself of its special identity and, in time, of its special destiny. The South since colonial times had always been a place apart, but it was not until the last years of the antebellum era that the differences were transformed from the regionalism natural to any vast territory into the intensely self-conscious sectionalism that finally led Southerners to believe they would be better off forming their own nation. The anti-slavery crusade was instrumental in bringing about that transformation, even though only the most radical of abolitionists contemplated the sudden manumission of slaves in the South. Here it was agreed that only a constitutional amendment, for which unattainable Southern votes would be necessary, could bring about emancipation.

But it was enough that, in the North, a vast consensus was growing in favor of slavery being limited to the states where it already existed. If that were done, so moderate anti-slavery voices argued, then as the free nation grew, slavery in the South would find itself isolated, unprofitable, and doomed for natural and peaceful extinction. Since the early 1830s, a large part of the pull of the West came from Texas, then still a province of the new nation of Mexico and a magnet for land-hungry American settlers from the slaveholding states of Kentucky, Tennessee, Alabama, Mississippi, and Louisiana. In 1836, these Anglo-Texans had won their independence from Mexico, and Texas stood as an independent nation for the next nine years until, under the guidance of President James K. Polk, from Tennessee, and his Secretary of State, John C. Calhoun, negotiations were successfully completed to bring about annexation to the United States. Texas President Sam Houston agreed, on the condition that United States troops were immediately dispatched to prevent Mexican attack. The treaty was signed on April 12, 1844, but due to Northern and abolitionist opposition to the addition of more slave territory to the Union, it was rejected by the Senate. Finally, in February 1845, the treaty was approved by joint congressional resolution, and Texas formally joined the Union.

But Texas was not the only place where American settlers, encouraged by the idea back home that it was the "Manifest Destiny" of the United States to extend from ocean to ocean, were ripe for joining the Union. In August 1845, John Slidell of Louisiana was dispatched to negotiate the purchase of New Mexico and California from Mexico and to secure a boundary for Texas that would reach to the Rio Grande. When he returned empty-handed in May 1846, Polk decided on war, and when, in May, General Zachary Taylor provoked an incident with the Mexicans, hostilities began. Abolitionists in Congress quickly labeled the war an attempt by Southerners to extend slavery.

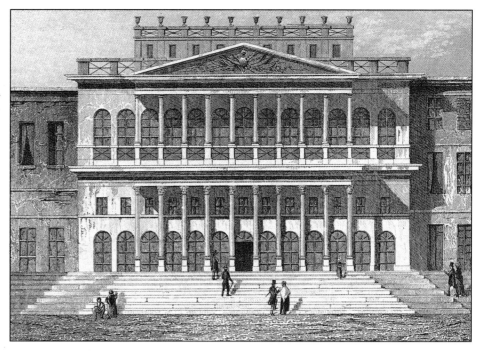

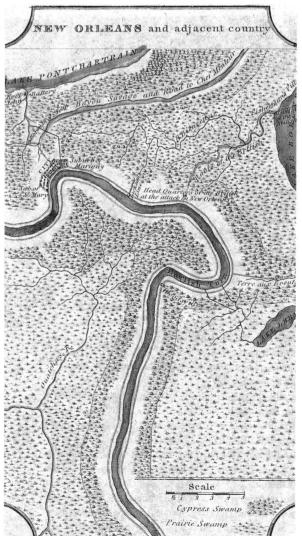

Above: *the St. Charles Theatre was built in New Orleans in 1835 but burned down in 1842. During the first half of the nineteenth century, New Orleans boomed, primarily due to its role as a trade outlet for Western farmers. In 1830-31 alone, more than 300,000 tons of freight were shipped to the city along the Mississippi River.*

Left: *an 1826 map of New Orleans and the surrounding region. By mid-century the port of New Orleans rivaled New York and Liverpool in shipping tonnage. Along with Charleston, Savannah, Galveston, and Mobile, all seacoast towns, New Orleans was one of the largest cities in the South before the Civil War.*

The Mexican War lasted a little less than two years and, militarily, was not a particularly glorious affair; the preponderance of American force rather than the brilliance of American strategy carried the day. The non-military consequences of the war were anything but minor, for with American victory came the addition to the American nation of a vast new territory, reaching all the way to the Pacific.

In anticipation of just such a likelihood, there was attached to a military procurement bill put before the Congress in 1846 an amendment written by a Pennsylvania Democrat and one-time Polk-supporter named David Wilmot. The bill was never passed, and so Wilmot's name went down in history attached only to a "proviso." But the "Wilmot Proviso," as it became known all across the land, became more famous by far than most laws, for it forced into sharp relief the question of slavery expansion and of the kind of America that was to be reproduced in the West. "Neither slavery nor involuntary servitude," it read, "shall ever exist in any part of said territory [to be acquired as a result of the war with Mexico], except for crime whereof the party shall first be duly convicted." At a stroke it proposed a bold approach to the problem of what to do with new territorial acquisitions, and at the same stroke it demonstrated how resurrected sectionalism could quickly shake the Union to its foundations. The national debate sparked by the Wilmot Proviso continued into the next administration, when North and South warily accommodated each other for the last time. That was in 1850, and for anyone who was listening there would be no better exposition of what, for the South and for other Americans, was finally at stake.

In the election of 1848, the Whig Party had regained the presidency by running a solid military hero of the Mexican War, General Zachary Taylor. Almost immediately, he was confronted with the problem of slavery in the Mexican Cession, comprising California, New Mexico, and parts of present day Arizona, Colorado, Nevada, and Utah. Since the end of hostilities in the spring of 1848, these areas had remained under military rule, and all of Polk's efforts to organize them had come to nothing. The problem was suddenly aggravated by the discovery of gold in California, whose population quickly grew to the level at which it warranted admission to full statehood without going through intermediate territorial status.

Taylor was not a subtle man, and to him it seemed a simple matter of inviting the Californians to write their own state constitution without Congressional authorization; in his view the Californians themselves should decide about the future of slavery in what was after all their state. This seemed simple, logical, and just. It was also naive, for at the end of 1849 there were fifteen slave and fifteen free states in the Union,

and the admission of California as a free state would upset that balance – so meticulously maintained since before the Missouri Compromise – for the first time and place the South in a minority position in both houses of Congress.

So the stage was set in the winter of 1849-50 for what would become known as the Great Compromise of 1850. The Congress that was elected in 1848, but which would not convene until December of 1849, was the body on which these burdens would now be placed. It still counted the old triumvirate of demigods in its number. Henry Clay of Kentucky was back after a long absence, and it was to this Henry Clay that the country looked as the "great pacificator"; past any real hopes of the presidency for himself, his words could be considered candid and honest. There was John C. Calhoun from South Carolina, the brilliant and belligerent defender of the South and her peculiar institution. And there was Daniel Webster from Massachusetts whose eloquence in defense of the Union has never been equalled before or since. Clay was seventy-three, Webster and Calhoun both sixty-eight, and Calhoun was dying of tuberculosis. This would be their farewell performance on the national stage. But some formidable younger men, whose time would come in the 1860s and 1870s, also sat in both houses. It was a Congress filled with names both already familiar and that would be heard from again. In the Senate there were, from Illinois, Stephen A. Douglas; from Mississippi, Jefferson Davis and Robert Foote; from Ohio, Salmon P. Chase; from Tennessee John Bell; from Virginia, James Mason; and from Florida, David Yulee. In the House there were, from Alabama, Alexander H. Stephens; from South Carolina, Robert Barnwell Rhett; and from Texas, Sam Houston.

The South had been quick to attack Taylor's plan for the quick admission of California as a free state, and it appeared that the Union might be on the verge of disintegration. But then in January of 1850, Henry Clay introduced a set of resolutions, proposed by Stephen A. Douglas's Committee on Territories, which attempted to cover all the points of North-South disagreement in one grand sweep. Clay proposed that California should be admitted as a free state on the basis of the popular choice of the people who lived there; that New Mexico should be organized as a territory without reference to slavery; that the Texas-New Mexico boundary dispute should be settled by the United States; that the slave trade in the District of Columbia should be abolished; that the Congress should have no power to interfere in the slave trade among the several slave states; and that a more stringent and enforceable fugitive slave law should be passed.

What followed was probably the greatest of great

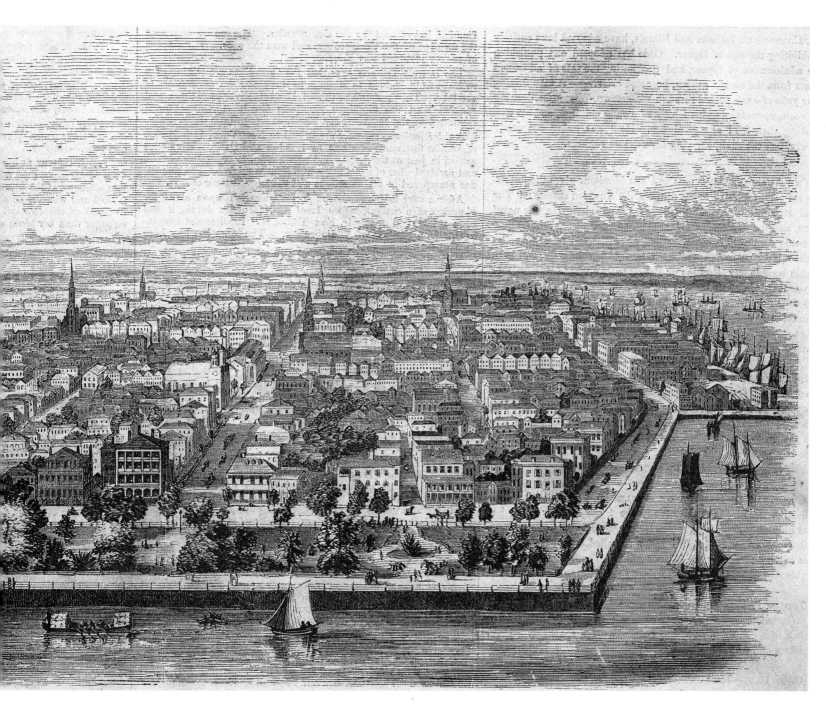

Above: *Charleston, South Carolina, in 1855. The city was home to many owners of large plantations, who preferred to live away from their plantations and allow their lands and slaves to be supervised by overseers.*

debates in the history of the Congress, and the speeches of the three old giants – Clay, Calhoun, and Webster – focused the issues sharply and impressed upon the nation the seriousness of the situation.

Clay spoke first, on February 5 and 6, 1850, and he spoke as a border-state Southerner with a message for both North and South. He appealed to the free states of the North not to insist on the Wilmot Proviso, but to rely on the dictum of nature and geography which, he said, would in fact keep much of the West free from slavery. He also asked Northerners to dampen abolitionist agitation and not to act against slavery in the District of Columbia. He sternly

admonished his fellow Southerners to stop wild talk of secession and deliberate disunion. He warned that secession could never be achieved peacefully and that it would not in any case insulate the South from its enemies. And he reminded Southerners that even though the South was losing control of the Congress, she still controlled the presidency and the Supreme Court, and that slavery could never be touched inside the South except by constitutional amendment, which seemed highly unlikely.

Clay was followed on March 4 by the cadaverous Calhoun, who would be dead before the month was out. His was the tortured, defensive voice of the

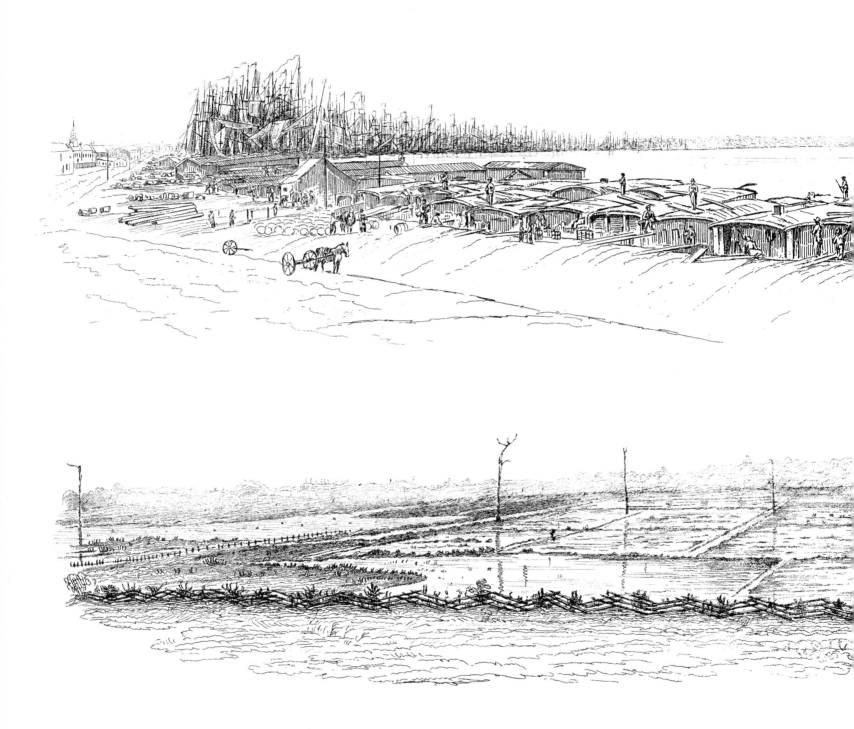

besieged South, heard for the last time from her most sparkling and partisan defender. Calhoun rejected Clay's compromise because he saw it, and rightly so, not as a solution but only as a truce. He argued that the sectional balance must be maintained, for with each additional tilt, the probability of secession increased proportionately. Under a new guise, he resurrected his old idea of the concurrent majority from nullification days, proposing a dual presidency,

one each from North and South, each with an absolute veto. Only this, he said, would guarantee equal power for the minority South. While he claimed still to be a unionist, the old Carolinian was actually saying that secession was a great possibility.

The last words came from Daniel Webster three days later. If Calhoun's was the tortured voice of the South, Webster's was the tortured voice not of the North but of the Union itself, which consisted of a

Top: an 1829 print of the docks along the Mississippi River at New Orleans. The Mississippi and its major tributaries, the Tennessee, Cumberland, Arkansas, St. Francis and White rivers, brought large-scale commerical trade to New Orleans.

tenuous mix of nationalism and sectionalism, freedom and slavery, North and South, East and West. "I speak for the preservation of the Union," he began. "Hear me for my cause." Like Clay, he warned Southerners against secession, saying it would not be achieved without violence. But mostly, the old New Englander leveled his sternest warning not at the slaveholders but at their Northern tormentors, many of whom were also his own constituents. Harshly, he condemned abolitionism and those Northern radicals who talked of eliminating slavery in the Southern states, and he threw his support behind Clay's proposal for a stricter fugitive slave law. Like Clay, he was beyond personal ambition and knew that his words would certainly bring down on his head waves of abuse, as indeed they surely did, from his own native section.

The last of these speeches was in March, but the final compromise would not be hammered out until September and would be the work of younger men. But the older men had come very close to the truth in their fears and predictions for the future of the sectional struggle. It was for their juniors to reap the whirlwind. During the summer of 1850, Stephen A. Douglas lined up the votes and painstakingly pushed the compromise through the Congress, piece by piece. Majorities were constantly shifting, with many Congressmen abstaining on offensive sections rather than casting no-votes. Moderate Southerners abstained on the provision to admit California as a free state; moderate Northerners abstained on the provision calling for a harsh fugitive slave law. President Taylor meanwhile resented the substitution of Clay's proposals for his own and perhaps would have vetoed the whole thing had he not died suddenly on July 9 after a short bout of cholera morbus. The vice president, Millard Fillmore from New York, was an ardent supporter of compromise and willingly signed the five laws that were finally passed between September 9 and September 20.

Basically it was Clay's compromise. California was admitted as a free state. The New Mexico Territory was to be organized without restriction on slavery, and when the time for statehood came, the people living there would decide the question. The Utah Territory received the same treatment. The slave trade in the District of Columbia was to be abolished on January 1, 1851. And a new fugitive slave law was to take effect, under exclusive federal jurisdiction. Under this law, special United States Commissioners were authorized, following a summary hearing, to issue warrants for the arrest of fugitives, with an affidavit signed by the claimant to be accepted as sufficient proof of ownership. Fugitives claiming to be free men were denied the right of trial by jury, and their testimony was not admissible as evidence.

Heavy fines were imposed both for marshalls who refused to execute warrants and for citizens who either prevented arrests or aided the escape of fugitives. Most offensive to Northern anti-slavery opinion was the provision of a $10 fee to commissioners for issuing a warrant against an alleged fugitive, whereas there was only a $5 fee for refusing one – a discrepancy viewed in the North as a bribe to let free blacks be kidnapped, carried South, and enslaved. Obviously, this part of the compromise was virtually unenforceable and shortly gave rise to a spate of "personal liberty laws" passed by the Northern states, which essentially claimed to nullify the Fugitive Slave Act within their borders. Once again, opinions depended on where a man stood, and the whole business demonstrated the fragility of the Union over the slavery issue as the 1850s dawned.

Most of the Southern states accepted "The Compromise." In Georgia, however, the governor called a special session of the legislature, and state representatives devised the "Georgia Platform," which declared that preserving the Union was secondary to preserving the "rights and principles it was designed to perpetuate." In addition, Georgia's lawmakers threatened secession if the Fugitive Slave Law were modified, if the interstate trade of slaves were banned, or if territories were denied admission to the Union because of the existence of slavery within their borders. In Mississippi, Unionists carried the day at a special convention called by the legislature to consider the Compromise. South Carolina's legislature backed the "Co-operationists," those who favored postponing a vote on secession until other states could be counted on to follow suit. Elsewhere, in Tennessee, Virginia, Kentucky, and North Carolina, the legislatures accepted the Compromise without offering threats of secession.

Despite its imperfections, the Great Compromise prevented Southern secession and saved the Union for eleven more years. Moderates in both parties deserved the credit. Although four Southern states – South Carolina, Georgia, Alabama, and Mississippi – called state conventions to discuss the results, only South Carolina showed a majority of disunionists. But the relief was short-lived. Flouting of the Fugitive Slave Law seemed a foul betrayal to the South; enforcing it seemed a sin to the North. After the long moratorium imposed by the Missouri Compromise, the issue of slavery expansion in the Louisiana Purchase soon reared its head again in Kansas and Nebraska. And the old system of two truly national political parties shortly disintegrated with the founding in 1854 of the Republicans, whose constituency was exclusively Northern and whose anti-slavery principles finally drove the Old South from the Union and to destruction.

Above: *rice fields in South Carolina, circa 1829. The cultivation of rice first came to South Carolina in 1696. Rice fields spread all along the tidal rivers and inlets, irrigated by water trapped in the fields by floodgates that opened with the rising tides.*

4

THE SOUTHERN NATION

Nations are built on the blood of patriots and on the ideas of clever and determined men. Both are moved by intense dissatisfaction with life as it is and by the conviction that old bonds of interest and affection, once a blessing but now a burden, must be severed for the sake of future generations. War frequently results, but if independence is achieved, then a new nation can be built. So it happened in the American colonies in the 1770s and 1780s, and so it began in the American South in the 1850s and 1860s. That the South failed to win its war for independence and failed to endure as a nation does not change the principle. But it does compel us to consider carefully the context for the South's effort to become a nation. For, in the very pattern of events and ideas that led Southerners to believe they could achieve independence lie the signs that help explain their final tragic failure to do so. During the 1850s, Southerners did not know that cataclysm would soon be upon them, but as the sectional controversy grew more intense, many Southerners boldly claimed their willingness to take such a risk. As it turned out, several of their key perceptions about the North – and about the South too – were badly flawed, though they seemed rational enough at the time.

The Great Compromise of 1850 left the Union unsettled. In the South, it encouraged talk of ultimate secession, something that was increasingly considered as a right. Given the triangular nature of the cotton economy, the main question that surrounded the secession debate was its expediency. The Compromise also helped to disrupt the Whig Party as a unifying national force and gave the one remaining national party, the Democrats, an increasingly Southern flavor. The fundamental issues at stake – the fate of slavery in the territories and in fact the fate of slavery itself – simply could not be resolved to the satisfaction of both sections in 1850, and efforts to resolve the same problems in 1860 led to secession and war. But the Compromise did delay secession for eleven years, and those years probably gave the North that edge in population, economic,

Left: *Abraham Lincoln speaks to the crowd gathered for the Lincoln-Douglas debate. During the widely publicized debate, Lincoln portrayed Stephen A. Douglas as a pro-slavery candidate; Douglas portrayed Lincoln as an extreme abolitionist.*

and manufacturing prowess that enabled it to win the war when war did come.

During the 1850s, the foundations for Southern secession and civil war were laid. But it is important to remember that the sectional conflict at the time lacked the irrepressible quality that it possesses in retrospect. At the time, most people probably did not believe the two sections were on an inevitable collision course, and most were concerned more with everyday living than with questions of high politics. National feelings coexisted with rising sectional feelings; intersectional bonds of friendship, family, and economic interest were substantial and exerted their power until the very end.

The Compromise of 1850 brought much divisiveness to the South in its wake. Southern Rights associations formed in Virginia, North Carolina, Alabama, South Carolina, and elsewhere to assert the South's right to secede, but the debate over that right was largely theoretical. Candidates nominated for office by South Rights Democrats in 1852 met with dismal results. Southerners were tired of the furor and, in general, wanted to give the Union another chance to redress the wrongs it had committed.

Nevertheless, the forces of sectional divisiveness increased even as the nation seemed to grow and prosper together. These had been seen to operate before, but as the controversy over slavery, in particular, grew hotter, they put new and greater strains on the bonds and sentiments of union. Economic determinism is now out of fashion, but the appearance that the North and the South presented of traveling down different and divergent economic tracks seemed real enough then. Although somewhat offset by the fact that Southern agriculture was in its greatest period of prosperity, economic issues were regarded at the time with great seriousness. The region's very prosperity, which gave substance to disunionists' descriptions of the South as the "wealth-producing" section of the country, gave plausibility to their cry that they were being exploited both by the unequal disbursements of federal revenues and by discriminatory legislation such as the tariff. At the same time, the prosperity of the 1850s encouraged many to think that, if need be, the South could in fact go it alone. Much was made of the extent of the region's direct trade with Europe and of the South's appearance of not being dependent on tight economic ties with the North.

For their part, non-Southern Americans – the burgeoning and diverse populations of the Northeast and the Northwest – were reaching their own consensus on economic matters with regard to the necessity of the protective tariff, a national banking system, and federally financed internal improvements. These were not new ideas, but ones that reached

PIERCE

back to Alexander Hamilton's economic program of the 1790s and to Henry Clay's "American System." Nor were they a new source of sectional friction. What was new was that impatient Northerners, who increasingly identified such a program as "progressive," interpreted opposition to it as part of an alleged "slave power conspiracy." Slavery alone, Northerners seemed to be saying – and not reliance on single-crop agriculture, which would have been more accurate – accounted for the South's economic "backwardness." Federal discrimination, Southerners responded, kept the South at a disadvantage. Both positions were simplistic and at opposite poles. And this is where the sectional debates of the 1850s differed from earlier ones: the room for compromise was rapidly diminishing.

The crisis in economic perceptions came in 1857 when the Congress passed a relatively low tariff,

Above: *Franklin Pierce was president when Senator Stephen A. Douglas from Illinois introduced the Kansas-Nebraska bill. A weak president, Pierce was unable to stem the tide of abolitionist fevor in the congressional halls.*

which was followed by a financial panic and recession. The North was hardest hit, which the South saw as proof of the superiority of its agriculture-based economic system and which confirmed in the minds of disunionists that the South could not just get along, but would actually be better off, without the North. Northern economic sectionalists said bad times were a direct result of reducing the tariff that painfully illustrated the high costs of trying to live in the same house with slaveholders.

The intemperate economic arguments that strained the union in the 1850s went hand in hand with perceived moral and cultural rifts. Demand rose in the South for Southern textbooks and Southern teachers and for the South to emancipate itself from literary dependency on Northern and European writers. The most tangible cultural bond had already snapped in 1845 when the two largest Protestant denominations in America, the Methodists and the Baptists, had divided over the slavery question into Northern and Southern groupings. In each case, the stigma of immorality was placed on the slaveholding South. But it was the publication of one particular book in 1852 – *Uncle Tom's Cabin or Life Among the Lowly* – that contributed to the course of disunion more than any other single cultural event. Author Harriet Beecher Stowe's experience of the South's peculiar institution was limited to say the least, but the impact of her novel was not. A member of a Northern anti-slavery family, Stowe drew heavily on the highly negative reports of conditions in the South to be found in Theodore Dwight Weld's propagandistic *Slavery As It Is*, and she reflected all its simplicities: overseers ("Simon Legree") were universally sadistic; slaves ("Uncle Tom") were angels in ebony; slavery was worse in the Lower South.

Above: *a political cartoon dated January 7, 1860, depicts Miss Columbia's attempts to gain control of her classroom in which the Southern students on the right declare, "Let us alone," and the Northern students on the left scuffle over New York senator William Henry Seward's "Irrepressibie Conflict" slate.*

While Stowe shared all the white racist attitudes of her time, slavery and not racial equality was her point, and she made it brilliantly. In the South, reaction to Stowe's book was vehement. Attacking the author and the book equally, newspaper editors claimed that Stowe had no knowledge of the conditions of slaves in the South, possessed no "moral sense," and had plagiarized Charles Dickens. The book achieved a permanent place in American literary history, but at that particular moment it also added the explosive element of moral self-righteousness to the slavery debate by strengthening the stereotype of slavery as a malevolent institution that stood, literally and morally, in the path of national progress. Thousands of Northerners, having previously held themselves aloof from the moral question, were swayed by the book to join the abolition cause.

Self-righteousness settled on both sides, as the South counterattacked the libel on its character with no less than fifteen novels of its own and with sweeping arguments that Northern wage earners were actually worse off than slaves. It was at this point that the South's criticism of Northern capitalism began to emerge in earnest, in the work of a Virginia lawyer, George Fitzhugh. In fiercely defensive works, *Sociology of the South* (1854) and *Cannibals All: Slaves Without Masters* (1857), Fitzhugh declared not only that Southern slaves were better off than Northern workers, but that the blessings of slavery should be introduced to the North where Northern workers would happily swap their illusory freedom for the slave's undeniable security. It was a fantastic argument that was recognized as such in the South, but anti-slavery, and increasingly anti-Southern, agitators in the North felt it gave currency to their suspicion that the South, if left unreformed, would enslave the rest of America.

The more bonds of economic interest and cultural unity that were snapped, the greater the pressure that was exerted on politics to hold the Union together. Ever since they had justified their revolt from Great Britain through the Declaration of Independence and then fashioned a functioning federal republic through the Constitution, Americans had exhibited a special genius for self-government, and by the middle of the nineteenth century they were surely more practiced at democratic politics than any other people in the world. But even their deftness, learned over many decades, at the art of the coalition and the slippery techniques of compromise proved unequal to the challenge that faced them. For as constitutionally abstruse as questions of majority rule and minority rights could be made to sound, by the 1850s there was nothing at all abstruse about their immediate manifestations. These were concrete, immediate, highly emotional, and ultimately beyond

the control of even the most brilliant political practitioners.

When compared with the generation of statesmen who made their last bows in the Compromise of 1850, "brilliant" is not a word that is easily attached to their successors. In the South, a new breed of political "fire-eater," who shared the dead John Calhoun's convictions but not the sparkle of his mind, took the stage, and while they did not dominate the scene, they made themselves heard ever more loudly as the decade progressed. Products of their time who knew how to take advantage of events, their language was heavy with powerful moral appeals and words like "principle," "oppression," and "destiny." The most eloquent was probably William Lowndes Yancey of Alabama, who, though once a unionist and denouncer of nullification, by the late 1850s was calling for the reopening of the slave trade and the formation throughout the South of "committees of public safety" to defend slavery, which amounted to an outright call for revolution. Robert Barnwell Rhett, a large South Carolina

Above: *James Buchanan served as minister to Great Britain while Congress was embroiled in the battle over slavery in Kansas. He won the Democratic Party nomination for the presidency in 1856 and went on the win the election.*

Above right: *Gettysburg, the first battle of the Civil War in which General Robert E. Lee was clearly defeated.*

Right: *a regiment of black soldiers during the Civil War. By the middle of the war, the Union Army needed more manpower, and various state governments organized regiments of black soldiers.*

slaveholder and ardent nullifier, had learned much from his mentor, Calhoun, but lacked Calhoun's early devotion to the Union. "Liberty and the Spirit of 1776" were his watchwords as he inducted the heritage of the Revolution into the service of the states' rights argument. In 1858, he proposed a constitutional amendment to protect slavery and said that if it could not be secured then the Union should be dissolved. Robert Toombs, a Georgia Whig, planter, land speculator and lawyer, began political life as a staunch unionist but ended a fire-eater. A man who moved slowly to the support of secession, once he had arrived he stayed committed until the end, and after the war was the most unreconstructed of old rebels. Every state had its fire-eaters: John Quitman and Jefferson Davis in Mississippi; Pierre Soule in Louisiana; David Yulee in Florida; Edmund Ruffin in Virginia. Ruffin – to whom went the honor of pulling the lanyard that fired the first gun of the Civil War and who, as prospects darkened for the South, blew his own brains out – was a rarity in moderate Virginia (which would be slow to leave

the Union even in 1861) and proclaimed himself an "adopted son" of South Carolina. No common pattern describes the background of these men, and they shared no one political ideology. But what held them together – an increasingly antique commitment to states' rights, white supremacy, the pro-slavery argument, and the South's and their own personal honor – were the same things that made for the foundations of Southern nationhood.

In the nation, North and South, politics through the 1850s grew steadily more sectional. In the wake of the Great Compromise, wedges of political separation broke apart the old national party system of Democrats and Whigs, and replaced it with two largely sectional parties neither of whose purpose was the preservation of the Union. Allegiance to the old parties never returned to its pre-1850 levels. Anti-slavery "conscience Whigs" fractured their party, and Southerner Whigs moved into the Democratic fold. In 1852, Franklin Pierce, a weak

northern Democrat sympathetic to the South, was elected to the presidency. Pierce's ill-advised efforts to buy Cuba from Spain alienated anti-slavery members of his party, who portrayed him as a sectionalist bent on the expansion of slave territory. Southerners meanwhile chafed at violations of the Fugitive Slave Law, which had been key to their acceptance of the Compromise of 1850. Northern attempts to nullify it with "personal liberty" laws led to Southern calls for strict federal enforcement and only confirmed what many Southerners had suspected all along: that the North had no intention of honoring the guarantees to slave interests that had been part of the Compromise.

It was however the very question that had compelled that compromise in the first place – slavery in the western territories – that now resurfaced to destroy it. Not until the South had actually lost the Civil War would that question be resolved again with such finality. Its resurgence in the early 1850s

Above: *Dred Scott, shown with his wife Harriet, sued the courts in Missouri for his freedom. He argued that his temporary residence in Illinois and the Wisconsin Territory, where slavery was outlawed, had made him free. The Supreme Court in 1857 stated that blacks were not citizens, thus they had no right to sue in federal courts, and that the Missouri Compromise, which prohibited slavery in the Wisconsin Territory, was unconstitutional.*

Right: *the Dred Scott decision was a focal point of Abraham Lincoln's debates with Stephen A. Douglas in July 1858.*

LINCOLN

was no surprise and was sparked by another, more benign fascination of that age, the railroad. With California in the Union, demand rose for a transcontinental line to reach from the Mississippi Valley to the Pacific Ocean. In the building of railroads, intense competition among potential termini was common, but in the case of the American transcontinental in the 1850s, ordinary civic competition was transcended by larger sectional ambitions and anxieties. In the old eastern America, the point at which the line would commence its 2,000 mile run across the new western America was deemed of great consequence in the now high-stakes contest for sectional supremacy. Chicago, St. Louis, Memphis, and New Orleans were all mentioned as contenders.

In the high political drama that ensued, Stephen A. Douglas, Democratic Senator from Illinois and chairman of the Senate Committee on Territories, quickly emerged in the leading role, and in Douglas it is possible to see something of the moderate North's workaday attitude toward slavery. It would be hard to characterize him, politically, as either pro- or anti-slavery, because he saw any such position as a political liability. A faithful Democrat, he was not unsympathetic to the South, and besides, he harbored presidential ambitions for which he would need Southern support. Personally he seems to have had no deep moral aversion to slavery, though he probably regarded it as an anachronism whose continued existence ran counter to the more progressive ideals of the age. Like many others, he believed slavery had largely reached its natural limits and would not easily extend itself into the new western territories no matter what the laws said; the Great Plains were simply not cotton country. He also believed in states' rights and extrapolated from this the notion of "popular sovereignty" as the best hope for organizing the western territories. By this, he merely meant that the settlers themselves should decide whether they wanted slavery or not, and that their decision about

Above: *a street scene in Montgomery, Alabama, in 1861. The State House is shown at the end of the street.*

Right: *"The Last Moments of John Brown," by Thomas Hovender. Northern abolitionists quickly seized the image of John Brown as a martyr to their cause.*

Previous page: *the first Battle of Bull Run in July 1861 brought a boost to the morale of the Southern troops. The Confederates under Beauregard pushed the Union troops from Manassas Junction back to Washington.*

Left: *the Battle of Sharpsburg, or Antietam, near Sharpsburg, Maryland, in September 1862, brought 70,000 Union troops against 40,000 Confederates. Both sides lost a combined total of 22,000 men. Confederate General Robert E. Lee used the cover of darkness to slip back into Virginia, and Union General George B. McClellan did not pursue the retreating army.*

Left: *a Civil War poster depicts Northern troops marching into the South in 1862. In reality, the Southern troops held their own that year, winning victories at the "Seven Days' Battles" and the second Battle of Manassas.*

Right: *Jefferson Davis of Mississippi was selected by Southerners to serve as president of the Confederate States of America. The West Point graduate often ignored administrative problems in order to devote his energies toward devising military strategy. He was generally too reserved to become a truly popular leader in the South, however.*

Above: *Northern troops under General Ambrose Burnside occupied Fredericksburg, Virginia, in December 1862, but they were no match for General Robert E. Lee's line of defense at Marye's Heights. On December 14, the Northern general ordered the evacuation of the city.*

Left: *John Brown, the martyred extreme abolitionist, remained a powerful symbol for Northerners during the Civil War. He was the focus of writer Robert Penn Warren's first published book,* John Brown: The Making of a Martyr.

it should be final. It was an idea with obvious appeal to the surging democratic spirit of the times, but one that unfortunately collided head-on with the Missouri Compromise, in which, thirty years before, the Congress, not the local population, had drawn its fatefully fixed geographical line across the Louisiana Purchase and allowed slavery to the south side, freedom to the north.

Douglas was a masterful politician and parliamentarian; he had been the person responsible

for shepherding Clay's Great Compromise through the Congress in the summer of 1850. But just four years later he misstepped to a colossal degree. The matter in question seemed urgent because of both the railroad and the consequent need to breach, by organized white settlement, the Indian barrier that could cut off hope of its construction. To that uncontroversial end Douglas proposed the most controversial of means – popular sovereignty – that lit the fuse of sectional controversy. Once and for all

Above: *the States' Rights Flag is unfurled by secessionists in Columbia, South Carolina, in December 1860.*

Right: *The* Charleston Mercury *announced South Carolina's secession in an extra edition.*

CHARLESTON MERCURY

EXTRA:

Passed unanimously at 1.15 o'clock, P. M., December 20th, 1860.

AN ORDINANCE

To dissolve the Union between the State of South Carolina and other States united with her under the compact entitled "The Constitution of the United States of America."

We, the People of the State of South Carolina, in Convention assembled, do declare and ordain, and it is hereby declared and ordained,

That the Ordinance adopted by us in Convention, on the twenty-third day of May, in the year of our Lord one thousand seven hundred and eighty-eight, whereby the Constitution of the United States of America was ratified, and also, all Acts and parts of Acts of the General Assembly of this State, ratifying amendments of the said Constitution, are hereby repealed; and that the union now subsisting between South Carolina and other States, under the name of "The United States of America," is hereby dissolved.

THE

UNION IS DISSOLVED!

his Kansas-Nebraska Bill of 1854 left the slavery question in those territories – both of which lay north of the 36/30 line laid down by the Missouri Compromise – to the decision of the people who settled there, though it did not specify when that decision should be made. Passed with the aid of Democratic President Pierce despite the opposition of Northern free-soil congressmen, the law voided the Missouri Compromise in the territory in question and, theoretically at least, laid the whole Louisiana Purchase open to the possibility of slave intrusion – if that was what local populations should say they wanted. The probability of that ever actually happening in much of the Great Plains was, everyone knew, fairly remote. But by the middle of the 1850s, the symbolism surrounding the slavery issue could overpower the facts. Southerners, who were initially not very interested in Douglas's bill because they were not very interested in Kansas or Nebraska as places to grow cotton, soon came to insist on their rights as American slaveholders to carry their slave property wherever they chose. Northerners, who knew they had no reason to fear that Nebraska would ever become a land of plantations, also attached much symbolic importance to being able to say America stood for the expansion of freedom, not bondage.

Douglas soon learned that he had created a political monster that wrecked his personal presidential ambitions in 1860 and which, by opening up the Louisiana Purchase to slavery, split the Democratic Party and set in motion forces that led toward war. There were two immediate consequences: "Bleeding Kansas," a proto-civil war in which American citizens, albeit in very small numbers, fought and died over slavery; and a massive political realignment that gave birth to a new Northern sectional party and further Southernized the Democrats.

As soon as the law had been passed, Kansas became the object of an intense sectional tug of war. In the North, a group of wealthy abolitionists formed the New England Emigrant Aid Committee to finance the movement of anti-slavery families to the Kansas territory. In the South, a few Kansas Associations were created as well to foster settlement by Southerners, but most of the men who made the move were poor and were attracted more by promises of acreage than by any desire to make Kansas a slave state. To keep the Northern settlers from winning local elections, Missouri settlers crossed the border into Kansas to vote at the polls. "Bleeding Kansas" came to the forefront of the slavery question as lawless bands of men roamed over the territory to assert their particular philosophy. By 1856 two competing territorial governments – one slave, one

free – were in operation. While there were never more than 200 slaves in the whole territory, Kansas became for Southerners a burning symbol of their rights, and for Northerners the epitome thus far of the moral struggle between slavery and freedom. To the young anti-slavery Republican Party, it became the greatest of campaign slogans on the way to putting Lincoln in the White House. The Congressional debates over statehood for Kansas were acrimonious and fruitless – admission, as a free state, came only in 1862, after the South had left the Union – but in one incident in particular, richly symbolic.

In May 1856, Charles Sumner of Massachusetts, the most outspoken abolitionist in the United States Senate, gave a speech entitled "The Crime Against Kansas" and in it used abusive and intemperate language about South Carolina Senator Andrew Butler. Two days later, Preston Brooks, a member for South Carolina in the House of Representatives, attacked Sumner with his cane in retribution. It took Sumner, supposedly, three years to recover, and his empty chair in the Senate became another dark symbol of the aggressions of the slave power. Brooks was held up as an example of how slavery blunted

Above: *at the Battle of Nashville in December 1864, a remnant of the Army of Tennessee under General John Bell Hood limped north toward the city after disaster a few days earlier in Franklin, Tennessee, where twelve Confederate generals were killed, wounded, or missing.*

Right: *the inauguration of Jefferson Davis as president of the Confederate States of America in Montgomery, Alabama. Davis was a native of Fairview, Kentucky, and moved as a child to Mississippi. After the Civil War and his release from prison, he wrote* Rise and Fall of the Confederate Government.

the moral sensibilities and inclined men to violence, a stereotype that was growing easy to believe just then. A move to eject Brooks from the House failed; he resigned and was then overwhelmingly re-elected.

The pressures of Kansas also proved too much for the Whig Party, which disintegrated as a national force after the Congressional elections of 1854. As with the emotional intensity that surrounded the issues of slavery and states' rights, so it is difficult today to recover a sense of meaning of the event at the time. The party system of Democrats and Republicans with which America functions today is essentially the same one that grew up in the wake of the 1850s realignment; and no one alive today has experienced the death of one of the two great parties. Such a death was not a casual occurrence and was not taken lightly. When the Whig party, then two decades old, could no longer contain its Northern and Southern members because of the slavery issue, a number of "anti-Nebraska" parties sprang up to fill the vacuum and became waystations for many Northern Whigs and free-soil Democrats *en route* to the new Republicans. The American or Know Nothing Party, which appealed largely to anti-Catholic and nativist sentiment in the North, also enjoyed a brief moment in the sun. In the South, however, the party's membership was generally composed of Whigs who were not eager to join the Democratic party.

But the future belonged to a new grouping – the Republicans. Not formally founded until 1854, the Republican Party gained strength with a speed that can only attest to vast unmet national hungers. The party, which just six years later would capture the presidency and effectively rule the nation for the next half century, came together from diverse elements of Northern society. There were temperance advocates whose demon was rum, and there were beer-drinking German immigrants; there were radical abolitionists, and there were moderate free-soilers who hated slavery and blacks with equal intensity; there were anti-slavery Whigs who supported a high tariff, a national banking system, and federal domestic improvements, and there were anti-slavery Democrats who abhorred those things. But the one principle that unified them into a powerful political force was opposition to the extension of slavery in the territories and the conviction that the Congress had a positive duty to prevent it. The party never advocated abolition but hoped slavery would die by containment. If emancipation were somehow to come about, then the problem of what to do with the freed blacks seemed as insoluble to Republicans as it did to Democrats and Southerners. Captive to their own fears of racial differences and the widely held conviction that the two races could not live in a state

of freedom in the same country, the Republicans never proposed anything more compelling than the old solution of colonization outside America. They did not pursue it with vigor but concentrated instead on the issue of the immorality of slavery and the unacceptability of its extension into the West. A mixture of pragmatism and idealism, of social and religious prejudices, the Republican Party replaced the defunct Whigs and soon successfully challenged the beleaguered Democrats for national power, and it did so as a purely sectional party of the North. There were no "Southern Republicans," and when the new party professed to speak for the nation, it spoke for a nation that excluded the South.

The attitude of the Republican Party toward slavery had much to do with Southern political behavior in the 1850s, and as the formula was carefully worked out by Republican politicians such as William Seward, Lyman Trumbull, and Abraham Lincoln, it expressed a caution that may seem surprising amid the highly charged emotions of the day. The Republicans avowed that they were a strictly "constitutional" party, which meant that, in their view, emancipation could only come about through state, not federal, action. And while they expressed their "moral aversion to the institution of slavery," they did not want to be mistaken as being friendly to blacks and so risk offending the majority Northern belief in the superiority of the white race. The Republican Party, they made clear, was the "white man's party" because it promised to keep the West free for whites and free from the presence of blacks, enslaved or not. The Democratic Party, they said, was the "black man's party" because it threatened to spread the pollution of slavery, and of the black presence, beyond the confines of the South. It was a very popular distinction at the time, for, as cleverly and honestly expressed by Republican leaders, it enabled constituents to vent their rage about slavery but retain their belief in the supremacy of the white race. When William Seward said in 1860 that blacks were inferior and incapable of assimilation into American society – and yet had a right to be free – he was speaking, without duplicity or self-deception, on behalf of thousands of moderate-minded Northerners.

Among the Democrats, who still controlled the Congress and the presidency throughout the 1850s,

Right: *after the Southern states seceded, many Federal forts were seized by the Southerners. At Fort Sumter, South Carolina, however, Northern troops still had control. When* *President Lincoln attempted to resupply the garrison in April 1861, the Southern troops opened fire on the fort. After thirty-four hours of bombardment, the Northern troops surrendered.*

Left: *at the Battle of Atlanta beginning in July 1864, Union General William T. Sherman led his troops to victory and then swept across Georgia in his infamous march to the sea.*

Below, left and right: *two views of General Robert E. Lee's surrender to General Ulysses S. Grant at Appomattox Courthouse on April 9, 1865. At the meeting between the two generals, the Northern victor stipulated that the Southern troops could return to their homes after laying down their arms.*

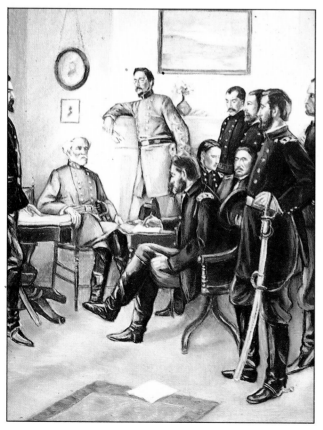

Above: *Confederate States of America president Jefferson Davis and his cabinet meet with General Robert E. Lee in Richmond. Richmond became the Confederate capital later in 1861. Alexander Stephens, vice-president of the CSA, is pictured second from the right.*

Northern party men shied from the question of the immorality of slavery but generally believed the institution stood little chance of spreading to the territories anyway. Beyond laissez-faire neglect, they possessed no solution to the race problem. Even more anti-black than the Republicans, many no doubt quietly regarded slavery as an evil, but a necessary one that served to keep freed blacks out of the North. For their part, Southern Democrats partook generously of the South's elaborate pro-slavery argument by the mid-1850s. For the purposes of national politics, it was their uncompromising stance that the Congress could not ban Southerners' special form of property from the territories and that the ultimate solution to America's race problem was already at hand: slavery.

The delicacy of the Democrats' position as a national party became apparent in 1856 when they nominated James Buchanan, a Pennsylvanian sympathetic to the South, for the presidency and

John Breckinridge, from the slaveholding border state of Kentucky, for the vice presidency. The platform, moreover, dodged the slavery question and pledged the party to the Compromise of 1850, the Kansas-Nebraska Act, and the principle of "non-interference." In doing so, the only remaining national political organization in America was admitting that, out of well-justified fear for its unity, it dared not take a position on the future of the most burning question of the day. The young but vigorous Republicans that year fielded the ardent expansionist John C. Frémont of California for president. Popularly known as "The Pathfinder," Frémont had made important explorations of the Oregon Trail, the Great Basin, and the Sierra Nevada. He ran on an openly sectional platform that denounced the repeal of the Missouri Compromise and upheld Congressional authority over slavery in the territories.

While the Democrats won one more time, the shape of the vote warned that something dire was

happening to the two major parties. A third party, the nativist Know-Nothings, had also fielded a candidate and carried one state, Maryland. The Democrats carried five free states – Illinois, Indiana, Pennsylvania, New Jersey, and California – and all of the South. The Republicans carried eleven free states and, with 1.3 million popular votes to the Democrats' 1.8 million, posted a remarkable first showing for a party just two years old. But as remarkable as the Republican's sudden strength was the sectional character of the vote. The one remaining national party, the Democrats, was shown to be disproportionately strong in the South. By the late 1850s, it would be reduced to an essentially Southern party with a Northern annex, which is what it would remain until Franklin Delano Roosevelt

fashioned a new Democratic coalition in the 1930s. The Republican Party, on the other hand, was a strictly Northern affair without any Southern annex at all and would remain so until the civil rights revolution of the 1960s finally broke the back of the Solid South.

The ensuing administration of James Buchanan was a stormy one that nearly buckled under the pressure of growing Southern political unity. The South's solidarity, though it was still far from uniformly disunionist, was a plausible response to the emergence and the successes of the Republican Party, which had brought home to all Southerners that they were faced with a moral crusade bent on the eventual but certain destruction of their way of life. When increasingly fearful Southerners

Above: *Union and Confederate dead litter the battlefield at Gettysburg in July 1863. Confederate losses at Gettysburg totaled 28,000; Union losses were 23,000.*

Right: *military supplies stored at Yorktown, Virginia. The industrial North had a huge advantage over the South in terms of military supplies.*

characterized all Republicans as "black abolitionists," they exaggerated grossly, but no more than did the Republicans who warned that the Southern slave power was determined to spread its special scourge all across America. Both sides soon began to believe their own propaganda, which, in one instance particularly, led to the South fatally miscalculating the balance of sectional power. For in the late 1850s, as troubled as the political landscape had become, the South's actual landscape of plantations and farms enjoyed enormous prosperity. For this reason, the myth that cotton was indeed king grew strong. This myth lent acceptability to the momentous decision to leave the Union by many Southerners who reasoned that a cotton-hungry Great Britain would have to support the South if she herself were to survive. But places other than the South grew cotton, and the only calculation that went into Britain's decisions about whom to support in the American Civil War was the cold calculation of who was most likely to win.

Each of the remaining three years of the decade brought grim omens. In 1857, the Supreme Court, five of whose nine justices were Southerners, waded into the slavery controversy with the Dred Scott Decision. The case involved the migrations of a black slave, Dred Scott, who during the 1830s had been carried by his master, John Emerson, an army surgeon, from the slave state of Missouri to Illinois, where the Northwest Ordinance of 1787 forbade slavery, and then to Wisconsin Territory, where the Missouri Compromise forbade slavery. Scott finally returned to Missouri and, in 1846, sued for his freedom on the grounds that his stay in free territory made him a freeman. The case in law involved three issues: whether Scott was in fact a citizen of the state of Missouri and thus entitled to sue in federal courts; whether his sojourn on free soil had made him a free man; and whether the Missouri Compromise, which prohibited slavery in the Wisconsin Territory, was constitutional. In a broad decision, the court seemed determined to vindicate the South and inflame the anti-slavery North. As a black and as a slave, the court decided, Dred Scott – and therefore all other black slaves and their descendants – was not a citizen and could not sue for his freedom. The court also found the Missouri Compromise, which had

Left: *the Battle of Shiloh in Mississippi resulted in huge numbers of casualties on both sides. The North lost 13,000 men; the South lost 10,700, including General Albert Sidney Johnston. The casualties were more than were sustained in the Revolutionary War, the War of 1812, and the Mexican War combined.*

Left: *At the Battle of Gettysburg in July 1863, Confederate general Robert E. Lee faced Union general George Gordon Meade, who had been given command of the army only a few days earlier.*

already been repealed by the Kansas-Nebraska Act, to be in violation of the Fifth Amendment to the Constitution, which prohibited the Congress from depriving a person of his property – in this instance, a slaveholder of his slave – without due process of law. With this interpretation, the court yanked from beneath the new Republican Party the chief plank of its platform: that it was the Congress's responsibility to restrict slavery in the West. The court was saying that the Congress had no such power. Some Republicans, in response, advocated disobeying the ruling; others, such as Abraham Lincoln, who had their eye on the larger game said the decision only emphasized the need for the Republicans to elect the next president, who could then change the composition of the Supreme Court by his judicial appointments. Southerners also fully understood that prospect.

In 1858, Kansas forced another rift in the Democratic Party when President Buchanan supported the admission of Kansas on the basis of a pro-slavery state constitution, which caused Stephen A. Douglas to break openly with both the administration and the Southern-dominated party. That summer, Douglas was challenged by Abraham Lincoln, his opponent in the Illinois senatorial race to a series of debates, which came to bear both their names and which laid before the nation – as if it wasn't already plain enough – the clarity of Republican conviction on the question of slavery and the impossible corner that Northern Democrats such as Douglas finally found themselves backed into. Was there any way, Lincoln asked Douglas at their debate at Freeport, Illinois, in August, to reconcile the Dred Scott Decision, which held that slavery could in effect go anywhere, with Douglas's precious

Above: *an 1865 photograph of Richmond in ruins. The city fell into Northern hands on April 3, 1865, despite General Robert E. Lee's attempts to protect it. Six days later, the Southern troops under Lee surrendered to General Ulysses S. Grant at Appomattox Courthouse.*

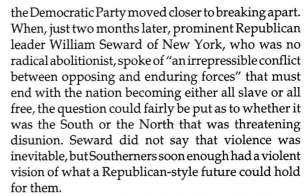

Left: *in "The Military Medallion," General Robert E. Lee is shown encircled by his staff. The Southern army was blessed with an abundance of well-trained officers, many of whom had graduated from West Point.*

Below: *Judah Philip Benjamin served as attorney-general in Jefferson Davis's cabinet. After the Civil War, he moved to England where he was engaged in a successful law practice.*

"popular sovereignty," which held it was the local population that must decide? Douglas's response became known as the "Freeport Doctrine," and in it he argued that, even in face of the seemingly sweeping Dred Scott ruling, the *de facto* exclusion of slavery could still be accomplished by the refusal of the local legislature to enact the police regulations, which only it was competent to do and without which slavery could not exist anyway.

A last resort argument it may have been, but the Freeport Doctrine was also very realistic in its assessment of the potential fragility of slavery in new and possibly hostile environments. Slavery did not travel well, which Southerners also knew but would not admit. Their reaction to Douglas's apparent betrayal was fierce, and just as Lincoln had hoped,

the Democratic Party moved closer to breaking apart. When, just two months later, prominent Republican leader William Seward of New York, who was no radical abolitionist, spoke of "an irrepressible conflict between opposing and enduring forces" that must end with the nation becoming either all slave or all free, the question could fairly be put as to whether it was the South or the North that was threatening disunion. Seward did not say that violence was inevitable, but Southerners soon enough had a violent vision of what a Republican-style future could hold for them.

John Brown's raid on the federal arsenal at Harpers Ferry, Virginia, in October 1859, had an irrational impact on the course of events that led toward the disruption of the Union and civil war. John Brown, destined to become a mythic figure in American history, may well have been a madman. Certainly his scheme to liberate a number of slaves whom he would then turn into guerrilla bands in the Virginia mountains had a bizarre quality about it, while his tactics in trying to carry it off suggest greater theatrical than military genius. His band of twenty-one included his own sons and several blacks. No local slaves came to their aid, as had been anticipated they might, and when a passing train alerted the outside world to their attack, Brown's raiders proved no match for the contingent of United States Marines, commanded by Colonel Robert E. Lee, who were sent to quell them. Over the course of late 1859 and early 1860, Brown and his surviving cohorts were tried for treason against the state of Virginia and for conspiracy to incite a slave insurrection and were hanged. But if their aim was to hasten the end of slavery in the South itself, as it surely was, then they could not have been more successful had they lived and won 10,000 slaves to their cause. For abolitionists promptly made a martyr out of crazed John Brown, and Southern fire-eaters had a field day proclaiming that this was but a foretaste of how the North intended to give substance to the "irrepressible conflict." Mainstream reaction, in both North and South, was initially more moderate: Lincoln, Seward, and Douglas all denounced the raid. But most Northerners, while disapproving the raid's methods, lauded its aims. Moderate Southerners, who responded slowly at first, moved toward the fire-eaters when it was revealed that Brown had not acted alone but had been financed by a secret cadre of wealthy Northern abolitionists. As extreme reactions set in on both sides, the raid became a turning point in the fast-developing secession crisis. Southerners who came to identify John Brown with the North – an oversimplification certainly, but a compelling one – concluded that they must secede to be safe, and the fear that moved them, thanks to John

Brown, was both real and immediate. All that was necessary now to drive the South to take the final fateful step was one more perceived aggression by the "Black Republican" Party.

This came in the election of 1860. The Democratic convention that year was poorly placed, in Charleston, South Carolina, and it was there that the Democratic Party formally and finally collapsed as a national body. Pro- and anti-slavery factions rancorously went their own ways. Northern Democrats later nominated Douglas on a platform of Congressional non-intervention in slavery in the territories. Southern Democrats, to whom Douglas was now anathema, nominated John Breckinridge of Kentucky on a platform of protecting slavery in the territories. The Constitutional Unionists, remnants of the old Whig and Know-Nothing parties, put up John Bell of Tennessee on a platform of upholding the Constitution and enforcing the laws. The Republicans, who convened in the booming new Western city of Chicago, forsook New Yorker William Seward who was associated with abolitionism in favor of Abraham Lincoln, a Western man from Illinois who had been born in slave-holding Kentucky and had done much to cultivate a moderate image. Lincoln's platform was a masterwork in its anticipation of the future economic development of the nation: it supported internal domestic improvements, including a railroad to the Pacific, and it called for a liberal foreign immigration policy and for a tariff to encourage industrial development. On the slavery question, it generously reaffirmed the principles of the Declaration of Independence and of the Wilmot Proviso and denied the power of the Congress or any legislature to legalize slavery in the territories. But it also reaffirmed the right of the states to regulate their own domestic institutions: the Republicans would not touch slavery in the South, however little comfort Southerners might take from such an assurance. It was an entirely sectional platform, utterly consistent with the party's ideology. Only Douglas ran a national campaign. He condemned the Republicans as a party of abolitionism and racial equality and warned of the dangers of electing a sectional president. Yet by emphasizing the danger that Lincoln allegedly posed to slavery, he paradoxically added fuel to the secession fire. Lincoln, for his part, did not make a single speech.

He didn't need to; the division of his opponents

Left: *the Union lines reform at the Battle of Sharpsburg, or Antietam, in September 1862. General George B. McClellan allowed a substantial victory to slip from his hands by refusing to pursue General Robert E. Lee's troops during their withdrawal into Virginia.*

made his victory highly likely. He carried every Northern state except New Jersey and not a single Southern one, but he garnered a plurality of just 39.8 percent of the popular vote. Douglas got twenty-nine percent, Breckinridge eighteen, Bell twelve. The sectional character of the voting was extraordinary, with Breckinridge and Bell (both Southerners) capturing eighty-five percent of the vote in the slave states, and Lincoln and Douglas (both Northerners) capturing eighty-six percent of the vote in the free states. The country thus had a Republican president, but no one could be sure what his mandate was. No party avowed abolition; no candidate in 1860 had called for secession. What was sure was that most Northerners were unwilling to see slavery spread and that they did not want the issue to become political. But for the first time, Southerners were faced with the fact of a sectional party in the White House and an avowed anti-slavery president.

South Carolina, predictably, responded first and, in December 1860, set in motion the train of secession. By February 6, 1861, all five of the other Deep South states – Mississippi, Florida, Alabama, Georgia, Louisiana, and Texas – had followed. The states of the Upper South – Virginia, North Carolina, Tennessee, and Arkansas – hesitated, but warned that they would resist any attempt by the federal government to coerce any state that left the Union. President Lincoln, in his inaugural address on March 4, attempted to walk a fine line aimed to preserve what was left of the Union and to reassure the South: "I have no purpose directly or indirectly to interfere with the institution of slavery in the states where it exists." But he also asserted that secession was legally not possible: "No state upon its own mere action, can lawfully get out of the Union." Both sides hesitated to make a move toward violence, and while the famous "first shot" was fired by the South, Southerners said it was in response to overt Northern aggression.

Coercion, or at least the appearance of it in the South's eyes, came in April 1861 when Lincoln, after much delay, attempted to resupply Fort Sumter in Charleston harbor, one of the few federal military installations in the Deep South that had not surrendered to state authority. The garrison commander, Major Robert Anderson, refused South Carolina's ultimatum, and at 4:30 a.m. on April 12 South Carolina forces commenced a bloodless bombardment of the island fortress. The national colors came down thirty-four hours later. The confrontation instantly galvanized the North in defense of the Union, and Lincoln issued a call for 75,000 three-month volunteers to put down the, as he put it, "insurrection." Lincoln's call for troops at last forced the hand of the states of the moderate border South: Virginia seceded on April 17, Arkansas on May 6, Tennessee on May 7, and North Carolina on May 20. Slaveholding Kentucky, Maryland, and Missouri did not leave the Union, but with their Southern sisters, they joined to declare the independence of a new southern nation, the Confederate States of America.

The Civil War was a war the likes of which Americans, or anyone else for that matter, had not seen before. It was the first real war of the industrial age; it was the first war in which armies were supplied by railway; it was the first war to be conducted by telegraph – and so able to be reported quickly to homefront populations; it saw the introduction of the observation balloon, the repeating rifle, an early form of machine gun, and, at sea, the iron-clad steam-powered warship. When it began in the spring of 1861, there was much talk on both sides of a quick and neat little conflict with the boys being home for a hero's Christmas. The more naive Northerners saw it as a mere police action to curb the recalcitrant South. Naive Southerners boasted that one dashing young Southern cavalier could whip ten cowardly abolitionists. More thoughtful men on both sides, including Abraham Lincoln and Jefferson Davis, understood that the sectional controversies of four decades had aroused deep passions and that in all likelihood, once the war had begun, the blood would flow until some final settlement had been achieved.

While neither side ever lacked the resolution to see the fight through to the bitter end, the North had the clear advantage in numbers and economic strength. The twenty-three Northern states contained a population of twenty-two million, which was augmented by heavy foreign immigration. The North could, even in a long conflict, replace its losses. Though heavily agricultural like the South, it had a more balanced economy with an advanced industrial establishment, strong financial institutions, an excellent railroad grid, a navy, and a merchant marine. The eleven states of the Confederacy had a population of some nine million, a third of whom were slaves. Its manufacturing was undeveloped and tied to agriculture; it had no substantial iron industry, and it made no heavy armaments. Its railroad network was still rudimentary and utterly unready for the massive load soon to be placed upon it.

Yet the discrepancy in resources, which Southerners recognized, was not initially compelling, for the South was taking a calculated risk on several counts: that the North would not actually fight to save the Union; that Great Britain and France, hungry for Southern cotton, would intervene on the South's behalf; and that the South's control of the Mississippi River would weaken Western support for the

Northern war effort. In each case the South guessed wrong.

The government of the new Confederacy got its start on February 4, 1862, in Montgomery, Alabama, where representatives of the six states that had by then seceded met at a convention. The representatives adopted a provisional constitution, modelled faithfully after the United States Constitution but specifically clarifying issues of States' rights that had become muddled over the past seventy years. They elected Jefferson Davis of Mississippi to

Above: *a Confederate sharpshooter lies dead in Devil's Den at the Battle of Gettysburg in July 1863. In November of that year, President Abraham Lincoln memorialized the site during his "Gettysburg Address."*

President and Alexander H. Stephens of Georgia to Vice-President. After his inauguration, Davis selected mostly conservative men to serve in his cabinet. The only ardent secessionist among them was Robert Toombs, Secretary of State. This lack of political sense on Davis's part resulted in immediate attacks by extremists. The lines were drawn between Southern nationalists and States rightists.

In military preparations, the Confederacy had some genuine advantages. Davis issued a call for a hundred thousand volunteers, and most who answered were well armed and clothed. In its officer corps, the Confederacy had Robert E. Lee, who had served as the superintendent of West Point and was attached to a Western command at the time of secession. Lee had been offered command of the Northern armies but had turned it down, resigned from the United States Army, and returned to his home state of Virginia where he was named major general of the Virginia troops. Other officers of the United States Army – Albert Sidney Johnston, Joseph E. Johnston, Samual Cooper, and more than 380 others – resigned their commissions and took new positions in the Confederate forces.

While Davis was engaged in fielding his new armies, dissension grew in the Southern Allegheny region of western Virginia and East Tennessee. The western counties of Virginia had not been represented at the convention that approved the State's secession. On June 11, 1861, Western delegates met at Wheeling to denounce secession and form a new government. The delegates elected Francis H. Pierpont governor, selected senators, and adopted a new state constitution for West Virginia, which was admitted to the Union in April 1863.

The residents of the Western counties were spurred to action by ancient grievances against the Tidewater government. In addition, they had hoped for industrial development in their region, richly blessed with coal and iron. More closely tied economically to the North, the West Virginians saw little hope of industrialization in the Confederacy so adamant against protective tariffs and federally funded internal improvements. They cast their lot with the Union.

In East Tennessee, only the establishment of martial law kept Unionists from following West Virginia's lead. Fierce fighting ranged throughout the mountain region, and Union sympathizers burned bridges to aid the Federal troops who had been ordered to the area. In August 1861, two Unionists were elected in the Confederacy's congressional elections. Thomas A. R. Nelson and Horace Maynard claimed that their elections were to the U.S. House of Representatives and set out for Washington. Confederate troops captured Nelson, but Maynard managed to travel to Washington, D.C., where he took his seat in Congress.

Fighting began in earnest in July 1861, as the Northern troops pushed from Washington toward Richmond. The Confederate troops under General Joseph E. Johnston and General P. G. T. Beauregard met at Manassas where Union General Irvin McDowell began an attack. The Confederates drew up along the small creek called Bull Run, forming a wall of resistance for which one of their commanders, General Thomas J. "Stonewall" Jackson, received his nickname. The advantage swung back and forth until at last the Confederates pushed the Union troops back into full retreat. Jackson pressed for permission to pursue the enemy, but the Confederate policy of defensive rather than offensive operations was maintained.

This early victory for the Confederacy was followed by disaster in the West. By June, the Union forces had wrested control of Kentucky, a State which had proclaimed neutrality in the War, Fort Donelson and Nashville on the Cumberland River in Tennessee, and Corinth, Mississippi.

Along the east coast, Southern cities were blockaded by the Union Navy to prevent the Confederacy from carrying on vital trade with Europe. By early 1862, the Atlantic Coast was completely under the Union's control, and blockades along the shore of the Gulf of Mexico were then begun in earnest. New Orleans fell on May 1, followed by Baton Rouge and Natchez. New Orleans, however, proved difficult to control. General Benjamin F. Butler was faced with a citizenry openly hostile to its Union captors. The women of New Orleans, having made a habit of insulting Union soldiers on the streets, were the target of Butler's "woman order," which proclaimed that any woman who insulted a Union soldier was to be arrested as a prostitute. Butler also seemed to disregard his soldiers' penchant for looting the heirlooms of New Orleans's families. Southerners calculated that most of the city's silverware was carted off by Butler's army, and they gave the hated general the nickname "Spoon."

While the Confederate Army suffered dismal losses in the West and along the seacoasts, it realized some success in the east. General Robert E. Lee's troops, entrenched around Richmond, faced Union forces under General George B. McClellan in the early summer of 1862. During the "Seven Days' Battles" at Mechanicsville, Gaines' Mill, Savage's Station, and Malvern Hill, Lee lost 20,000 men and McClellan lost 16,000. Richmond was saved, however. Lincoln remained determined to capture the Confederate capital and sent 50,000 troops under General John Pope into Virginia. Lee's troops routed the new Union Army at the second battle of Manassas,

Below: *the procession during the funeral of President Abraham Lincoln. Less than a week after General Robert E. Lee surrendered at Appomattox Courthouse, President Lincoln was killed at Ford's Theater. With his death, the South lost any chance it had for a compassionate peace.*

and Lee began preparations for an invasion of the North.

The Confederate's push was successful at Harpers Ferry, but at Sharpsburg, Lee lost 8,000 of his 40,000 troops. With no hope of reinforcements, he withdrew across the Potomac and maintained his position at Fredericksburg. On December 13, Union troops under General Ambrose Burnside attacked. Over the next two days, the Union lost 12,000 men and ultimately was forced to withdraw.

The Union Army's humiliating performance in the East that summer, combined with increased pressures from abolitionists, influenced President Lincoln to change the purpose of the War to the preservation of the Union. In September 1862, he issued the Emancipation Proclamation, which freed all slaves in states in rebellion after January 1, 1863. In effect the law freed no slaves at all. It did not apply to the states that had already fallen to Union control, and in those states still actively fighting, the United States government had no jurisdiction. In the South, the Proclamation increased support for the

Confederate government, and even those people who had opposed secession now rallied to the Confederate cause.

The year the Proclamation went into effect brought sweeping losses to the Confederate Army. Vicksburg fell to the Union after a prolonged siege in the summer of 1863, and when Port Hudson fell a short while later, the entire Mississippi River was in Union hands. After a victory at Chancellorsville, Virginia – a victory made less bright by the death of Stonewall Jackson – the Confederate Army marched into Northern territory. At Gettysburg in early July, the Confederate troops displayed stunning gallantry but were forced to retreat after sustaining heavy losses. To the south, the Confederates were at first successful at the Battle of Chickamauga, and they surrounded the Union Army in Chattanooga. The arrival of General Ulysses S. Grant, who devised a plan to break the Union Army out of the city, kept the Confederates from claiming victory. Instead they were forced to retreat into Georgia.

The following year, some brief moments of victory came to the Confederacy. In the region called the "Wilderness," General Lee's army outmaneuvered General Grant's forces time and again, but unlike the Union generals who had faced Lee earlier in the war, Grant did not withdraw from his push toward Richmond. He pressed on to Cold Harbor, losing 55,000 men to Lee's 19,000 along the way. But the Confederacy's elation over the saving of Richmond was darkened by the prolonged siege of Atlanta, which fell to General William T. Sherman on September 3.

Sherman then began his march across Georgia toward Savannah, plundering the countryside along the way. When Savannah fell on December 20, the Confederacy was cut in two. The government in Richmond could maintain communications only with troops in Virginia and North and South Carolina. Sherman then pushed north through the Carolinas toward Raleigh. Grant and Sheridan pushed toward Richmond and gained control of the city on April 3. Lee's army was surrounded, and on April 9, he and Grant met at the home of Wilmer McLean in Appomattox. Lee surrendered his 28,000 troops after receiving terms from Grant that would allow his men to return to their homes. President Davis fled from Richmond in hopes of meeting up with Johnston's troops and encouraging them to continue fighting. The cause was hopeless, however, and Johnston surrendered in North Carolina later in April. The armies in the Deep South and west of the Mississippi followed suit in May. The Confederate President continued his flight, now toward Mexico, but was captured on May 10 in southern Georgia and was carried to Fort Monroe.

The physical costs of the Civil War were enormous on both sides. The War killed between 600,000 and 700,000 young men in a nation totaling only thirty-three million: a fatality rate approximately double that suffered by American forces in both world wars in this century. The nation, North and South, lost not only these men, however, but the children and the grandchildren who never were, a cultural loss that is beyond calculation. The South lost the most physically: its cities, towns, and plantations were devastated and its economy ruined. During its brief and turbulent existence, the Confederacy, which had failed to stay the ruin and establish Southern nationhood, had yet crystallized Southern distinctiveness. It left Southerners with a heritage as peculiar as the one slavery had first given them. In their epic bid to secure their independence and preserve slavery, they exceeded their strength – and perhaps the strength of any people trying to defend such an anachronism, even in the staunchly race-conscious nineteenth century. For their presumption, history judges that they deserved to lose. For their defense of liberty against the centralizing power of the national state – a moral and political stance originating in the seventeenth and eighteenth centuries and one which tragically fell into some disuse in the twentieth – the Confederate Southerners merit a kinder judgment.

5

THE SURVIVING SOUTH

The end of the old order, and of the beliefs and institutions upon which it was based, was guaranteed by the military outcome of the Civil War. But the pace of their demise was slow and unsteady. During the first postwar years, the period known as the Reconstruction, the South was decisively acted upon by the world outside itself; most dramatically, a new system of race relations was promulgated but hardly consummated. The aims of the Northern reformers were embodied in laws passed in Washington, D.C., following which the full weight of the nation was brought to bear in a concentrated effort to coerce Southerners into different ways of believing and behaving.

The unfortunate implication of this story as it is usually told, however, is that South and Southerners were merely passive objects in this process. There were real people in the South, many of whom were not terribly happy either about the outcome on the battlefield or about the determination of the Radical Republicans to "wage the peace" as vindictively as Grant and Sherman had waged the war. And there were thousands of freed slaves – freedmen – for whom life in the South in the decade after Appomattox brought a mix of freedom, tragic insecurity, and hardship. These were years of radical change, but they were also years of surprising stability. And they were years when most people's concerns remained the primary ones of maintaining peace and achieving a degree of civil order and security, of keeping body and soul together, and of somehow living decent lives according to the standards their God, their fathers, and their fellows had taught them.

The tags for the period 1867 to 1876 are various – Congressional Reconstruction, Radical

Left: *the Senate during President Andrew Johnson's impeachment hearings. When Congress passed the Tenure of Office Act in 1867, the president refused to abide by the new law. He dismissed his secretary of war, and Congress immediately set in motion the impeachment process.*

Reconstruction, and "Black Reconstruction," the ultimate phrase of opprobrium, especially for many white Southerners who perceived these as the worst of all possible times. The words "Black Reconstruction" are also misleading. In the literal sense, it was black only in that votes of the freedmen placed white men in control of Southern state governments. Officeholders of this period remained predominantly white, though they owed their offices to black and, to a smaller extent, carpetbag and scalawag votes. With a few notable exceptions, blacks held only minor posts. Fourteen served in Congress, six held lieutenant governorships, and eight served in state cabinets. Between 1868 and 1874, blacks outnumbered whites in the South Carolina house, but whites controlled the senate and the other branches of the state's government. In Mississippi, where blacks constituted the majority of the population, there were seventy-five whites and forty blacks in the first Reconstruction legislature. In Florida, which was forty-five percent black, only nineteen blacks went to a seventy-six man legislature.

Black political participation was superficial even in these extraordinary circumstances and thus foreshadowed the Southern pattern for decades to come. There was much more black voting than officeholding, the latter the object of fierce white resistance. Participation was superficial in another sense, for while thousands of freedmen may have cast ballots and a few may have held office and tasted power, for the great mass of blacks the years of Reconstruction saw no really serious and determined effort to restructure the South's economy so that black Southerners would have a chance of lifting themselves out of the mudsill position where antebellum theory and practice had left them. They discovered that you can vote all you want and hold office here and there, but if the reins of economic power stay beyond your reach, then gains that seem momentarily so glorious fade quickly enough. So it was in the South. Economic power remained firmly with the whites, and in a region that had been devastated by war and where there wasn't a lot of wealth to go round, it sadly followed that the ones who ended up with the least were the former slaves.

There was social change to the extent that the races mingled in some public places where the relation between them was no longer that of master and servant. Yet there was never any real possibility that actual control of the South would pass to the blacks, unless there was massive and punitive confiscation of white property, followed by its redistribution to blacks, and accompanied by an equally punitive disfranchisement of former Confederates. Most whites who were not consumed with mindless paranoia knew this would not happen. They knew

that if economic and social control remained in their hands, then the Radical experiment in black political participation could not be sustained forever. Such participation was more than enough to fire the most basic kind of anger in whites, who were absolutely convinced that blacks were simply not entitled either to any political power at all or to the slightest measure of social equality. To whites, Reconstruction was a period of alien government imposed from the outside by Northerners, a government that invited the participation, if not predominance, of the alien race in their midst. To them, Reconstruction represented a direct, if incomplete, assault on white supremacy in the South, and it raised the issue, and raised it boldly, of how to regulate relations between the races. By the end of Reconstruction, which brought the restoration of local white political control in all the Southern states, this issue seemed to have been permanently resolved. In fact, it smoldered beneath the surface of Southern life for a century and more.

As the Confederacy crumbled and the Union took control of region after region in the South, President Lincoln was determined not to direct malice toward the conquered people. Despite heavy opposition in his Republican Party, the President devised a "Proclamation on Amnesty and Reconstruction." This plan called for the restoration of civil rights to all Southerners, except highly ranked civil and military officials, after they took an oath of allegiance to the Constitution. The plan also specified that when ten percent of the state's voters had taken

Above left: *the Radical Republicans failed by one vote to impeach President Andrew Johnson. On May 16, 1868, the hearings concluded, and a few days later, the Republicans nominated General Ulysses S. Grant as their presidential candidate.*

Above: *Vicksburg, Mississippi, after the Civil War. The First Reconstruction Act, which passed Congress on March 2, 1867, divided the former Confederacy into five military districts administered by a major general. Only by adopting new constitutions that guaranteed the right to vote to blacks could the states rid themselves of military rule.*

the oath, the state could then re-establish a government.

Congressmen Henry Winter Davis and Senator Benjamin Wade then took the reins of two new Congressional committees created to deal with the question of reconstruction. Their work, the Wade-Davis Bill, went far beyond the President's plan in terms of punishing the rebel states. The bill required fifty percent of a state's voters to swear allegiance before the resumption of state government, called for the states to revise their constitutions to abolish slavery, and disfranchised all Confederate military officers ranked Colonel or higher.

President Lincoln did not sign the radical Wade-Davis Bill but allowed it to fall victim to the pocket

veto when Congress retired. Neither the President's plan nor the Congressional bill had been signed when, on April 14, 1865, John Wilkes Booth assassinated Lincoln at Ford Theater. With Lincoln's death the reconstruction debate fell to President Andrew Johnson.

Johnson, a former tailor from North Carolina and then Tennessee, was a self-educated man who had slowly risen through the ranks of political office from alderman to U.S. Senator. He had retained his seat in the Senate after Tennessee seceded – the only Southern Senator to do so – and after the fall of Nashville, President Lincoln had appointed him military governor of Tennessee. Johnson's plan for reconstruction was announced on May 29. It included

all the provisions of Lincoln's plan but added that individuals with property valued at $20,000 or more were excepted from amnesty. In this way, Johnson attempted to radically alter Southern society. No lover of the white planter class, Johnson wanted to make room for small farmers and poor whites in the Southern political scene.

Southerners who were denied pardons under Johnson's general amnesty plan could apply directly to the administration upon receiving recommendations from prominent citizens or military officers. The applications were first approved by the United States attorney general and were then forwarded to the president. In all, Johnson approved 13,500 of the total of 15,000 applications for pardons. Half of the applications approved by the President were submitted by individuals who held more than $20,000 worth of property.

Congress was not satisfied with Johnson's plan. The Radical Republicans ignored the reorganized state governments and between March 1867 and March 1868 passed four reconstruction acts. The first organized the Confederate states into five military districts to be policed by the army. The second

required the commander of each district to compile a list of voters who had taken an oath of allegiance. This law also specified the mechanism by which the states and their voters would draft and ratify new constitutions. The third law gave the registration boards absolute power to grant voting rights or withhold them. These boards, it has been estimated, disfranchised 150,000 white Southerners, and no appeal process was allowed.

In 1867, delegates were chosen to serve at constitutional conventions, and their work was put to vote in all the Southern states except Virginia and Texas in early 1868. Many white Southerners stayed away from the polls, and because the second Military Reconstruction Act specified that one-half of the registered voters had to participate in the ratification, their absence from the polls was in effect a vote against the new constitutions. In a reaction against the white Southerners' resistance to participation, Congress then passed the fourth Military Reconstruction Act, which repealed the provision that required one-half of the registered voters to cast ballots in the ratification process. With the passage of this act, all the Confederate states, except Virginia,

Above: *after the Civil War, Richmond, Virginia, shown here, and the rest of the South were desperately poor. After drafting a new constitution, the state of Virginia was readmitted to the Union early in 1870.*

Right: *Charleston, South Carolina, circa 1880. Although manufacturers in the South increased production during the Reconstruction years, the percentage of national output claimed by the South declined. The South was striving to improve its station, but the North advanced much more quickly.*

Mississippi, and Texas were readmitted to the Union. Virginia and Mississippi later ratified their constitutions and were readmitted in early 1870; Texas completed its constitution and was readmitted in March 1871.

With the exception of Virginia, where Conservative Democrats won control, the Reconstruction governments were Republican governments. In ten states, Republican rule lasted anything from one to nine years – one in Georgia, nine in South Carolina. Judging their accomplishments and failures has been a touchy question over the years. For years afterward, most white Southerners couldn't say enough bad things about these regimes, and it became a sacred part of Southern myth that Reconstruction constituted the "blackout of honest government" and the supreme and unforgivable insult to the white race. Others – literate blacks and Radical partisans – recalled it as a noble and well-intentioned experiment in which the native virtue and sterling performance of the blacks was matched only by the unadulterated malice of their Southern white adversaries.

Part of the reputation of the Republican regimes is notorious, particularly the alleged corruption among Republican officeholders. Sure enough, the record bears out that it was something of a picnic for grafters great and small. Stories were reported, and some verified, of blacks in South Carolina voting large appropriations for brass cuspidors, expensive cigars, and gifts for wives and girlfriends. In actual fact, the blacks reaped very little of the largesse of corruption, not because they were more virtuous than the whites, but because there were fewer of them in positions offering the opportunity for corruption. Most officeholders were whites, and they bear the greatest responsibility for the fraud and corruption of these years. One of the richest fields for such activity was the Southern railroad system, left in a shambles by both armies, which everyone agreed had to be quickly rebuilt. Every Southern state except Mississippi permitted state aid to the railroads, a disposition in which imaginative grafters saw great possibilities and from which they reaped great rewards.

But in matters of corruption it is important to keep in mind that the weakness was not limited to Republicans, and that after the South was returned to native white rule in the 1870s, financial probity was not the hallmark of the restored Democratic regimes. Nor was government corruption in these

Right: *a Southern legislature during the Reconstruction period. Many of the Republican administrations elected in the South were corrupt, but some good was achieved, and the state constitutions redrafted during the period were more democratic than their predecessors.*

Above: *a black man hanged after being accused of raping a white woman in West Virginia circa 1880. By the mid-1870s, many Northerners lost interest in avenging themselves on the Southern rebels, and Southern blacks were left to fend for themselves in the hostile South when the Reconstruction armies were withdrawn.*

and public schools, never a strong point in the South, got their first government boost, but it cost money. Tax rates naturally went up to pay for new services.

For all their ineptitude, the Republican governments in the South did more than take bribes and swindle the taxpayers. Even though the presence of blacks in public office would soon pass away, these regimes made marks that would last longer than they did themselves. The state constitutions on which they rested were superior to, or at least more modern than, their antebellum predecessors. Participation in politics was broadened to universal white manhood suffrage. Even blacks, now guaranteed the vote by the Fifteenth Amendment, usually favored the vote for all whites regardless of the latters' past association with the Confederacy and the defense of slavery. The new constitutions asserted the right of children to schooling and the new state governments backed this up with appropriations that at least began to support such institutions. These administrations also began to give some tentative legal protection to women, who in much of the region had until this time to rely pretty much on their wits and their sex to get along in a man's world. They also did what they could to promote the economic rebuilding of the South, though in this they were severely limited by powerful prevailing notions about the limited role the state should play in the economy. They established both agencies to promote immigration into the South and, especially important, programs to promote industrialization. And of course these were the governments that for the first time gave blacks a real, though limited, chance to show what they could do in positions of power, trust, and responsibility. The record of this effort is obviously mixed; crooks and chiselers mixed with honest and capable public servants. The first black man to sit in the United States Senate was Hiram Revels, an ordained minister and a schoolteacher from Mississippi. Revels was the first black to fill the chair once occupied by Jefferson Davis, and he was followed by another black, Blanche K. Bruce, who had been born a slave in Virginia, escaped bondage to become a teacher, and then returned to the South in 1869 to settle in Mississippi. Blacks from Florida, Louisiana, Mississippi, Georgia, North and South Carolina, and Alabama served in the United States House of Representatives, and while not all of their careers in public life were especially memorable, neither were they any less remarkable nor any more prone to corruption than those of many of their white counterparts.

years an exclusively Southern phenomenon. Nationally there were far more egregious examples of public wrongdoing: the Democratic Tweed Ring in New York City, and the byzantine affairs of the entire Grant Administration between 1869 and 1877. Traditional critics of the Reconstruction governments also point accusingly at vastly increased public expenditures – extravagance became the catchword – and rising state debts as evidence that these were governments composed of the selfish, the shortsighted, and the morally depraved: carpetbaggers, scalawags and blacks. But perspective demands that we acknowledge that even if these regimes spent more, and they did, than their antebellum predecessors, they also did more. Officeholders now had to be paid more than a token;

But the story of Reconstruction in the South is only part of the story, for better or worse, of the Republican regimes in the state capitals. The South

was not just a place being acted upon, but was a place filled with people acting on their own behalf to maintain their values and assert their influence on the nation. Whatever Reconstruction did or did not accomplish, it was the result both of Radical planning and action, and of Southern obstruction and reaction. The South may indeed have been prostrate at the end of the war in 1865, but the sinew of the white South had not been broken. Most white Southerners repudiated secession and knew they were now in the Union for keeps, but as the property owners with the economic power, they were not about to automatically jettison their traditional ways of thinking and behaving. They did not change their fundamental notions of how society is and should be put together. They did not change their religion, and

they did not change their racial prejudices. Most of them were not fools but survivors, who knew that time was on their side and that the North would eventually tire of its moral crusade to refashion the domestic life of the wayward South. By the middle of the 1870s, as Southerners sensed that weariness coming on, they increased their resistance and sent a message to Washington that was unmistakable: restore home rule and with it white supremacy.

From today's perspective, in the wake of the civil rights movements of the 1950s and 1960s, it is easy to look back on the white Southerners of the Reconstruction era with contempt for a people so morally dulled as to sabotage such a noble experiment in racial justice. But viewed by the standards of that age, it was they and not their reformist antagonists

Above: *Hiram Revels from Mississippi takes the oath of office as a senator from his state on February 25, 1870. The first black to be elected to the Senate, Revels was an ordained minister and schoolteacher. The seat he filled in the Senate had once belonged to Jefferson Davis.*

Above: *the opening of the convention of the National Cotton Planters' Association of America at Progress Hall in Memphis, Tennessee, in 1881.*

Left: *Federal troops occupy the State Capitol of South Carolina, circa 1876. The presidential election of that year provided the occasion for the South to rid itself of the Northern-dominated state governments. When the election results were contested, Southern Democrats vowed to back the Republican Rutherford B. Hayes in return for his promise to withdraw troops.*

who represented the American mainstream; it was the Radical Republicans' ideas about the proper role of the government in social matters and their ideas about the necessity of racial equality as mirrored in the Civil Rights Act, the Fourteenth and Fifteenth Amendments, and the Reconstructions Acts, that were really quite exceptional and out of step with the times. In the 1860s and 1870s, they were the ideas of social visionaries and evangelical moral crusaders, who had understood the ultimate implications of the Declaration of Independence, and it is easy to applaud them because their ideas appeal to the modernist egalitarian sensibility. But it would be a mistake to believe that those ideas must have made the same good sense over a century ago. To white Southerners at the time, such ideas were radically dangerous and subverted everything they had been taught to believe made for the good life.

White Southerners' views about the proper role of the state in society, their ideas about race relations

as mirrored in their resistance to Reconstruction, their "redemption" of the South, and their subsequent rule over the region for the next eighty or ninety years were the widespread cultural currency of much of the western world. These were men convinced of the absolute impossibility of the black and white races coexisting in one place, except in a relationship of complete white control and complete black submission. Their commitment to white supremacy sprang from tradition, and in the 1870s and 1880s, it was also bolstered by the best scientific opinion. Herbert Spencer and William Graham Sumner pioneered a fierce brand of social Darwinism that dovetailed nicely with the practice of white supremacy at home and abroad. White Southerners were not alone; they were not an isolated, embattled minority of evil people who somehow never outgrew nasty habits of whipping their slaves and keeping millions of blacks in their place. And the blacks themselves knew this too.

In the immediate aftermath of the war, the first white Southern attempt to define the new relationship between black and white resulted in the Black Codes, which were harsh but also understandable. The codes were an attempt to define the legal status of the freedmen, who were as yet unprotected by the Fourteenth Amendment and its citizenship provisions. At first glance they resembled the old slave codes of antebellum times, but they were actually more like the old laws that had governed the status and activities of free blacks under slavery. Freedom did not in itself confer citizenship, nor did it define a man's rights in society. In both tradition and the common law, the determination of the rights of citizens, matters of crime and punishment, marriage and divorce, and so forth form civil and criminal codes relating to a particular group of people, and in this country the formation of such codes had always rested with state governments. In the antebellum North and South, the free black had been very much a second-class citizen who lived under restrictive laws laid down by whites. After the war, however, the South was confronted with an immediate and enormous increase in the numbers of "free persons of color," whose status had somehow to be defined and controlled. The Black Codes were the initial, almost instinctive, response to this need.

Mississippi's legislators passed the first code – a severe one, as would be South Carolina's – in 1865, and it was clearly aimed at maintaining white supremacy in a part of the South where blacks

outnumbered whites. In states with clear white majorities the codes were less harsh, but all of them attempted to regulate black social behavior and economic activity. In every case, special penalties were stipulated for black vagrants and for those who broke their labor contracts. Racial intermarriage was prohibited; segregation was attempted. In the short run the codes were a blunder on the part of the white South because they caused an angry reaction in the

Above: workers pick through and sort tobacco leaves. Below: Workers spin tobacco into plugs. After the Civil War, the South remained predominantly rural, and those industries that developed, such as tobacco manufacturing, were

primarily tied to agriculture. The new popularity of the cigarette during the Reconstruction period and the introduction of bright-leaf tobacco provided the tobacco industry with a much needed boost.

North, where they were interpreted as an attempt to reimpose *de facto* slavery. They provided Radical Republicans with the arguments they needed to convince Northerners that a harsh Southern policy was necessary: the Civil Rights Act and the Fourteenth and Fifteenth Amendments were passed as a consequence, and all the legal realities were suddenly changed. But the principles behind the codes and some of the general policies they embodied were

destined for long and influential careers, and in the years after the South had been returned to local white rule, shadows of the Black Codes would reappear as evidence of white determination that the children of American black slavery should remain perpetual serfs and servants. It was a caste system based on the subordination of blacks in an inferior social and economic position and demanding their complete elimination from politics.

The means available to achieve that end were various, but the most obvious was violence, which was practical because the South never felt the heel of an overwhelmingly powerful army of occupation. The actual number of federal troops occupying the post-bellum South was never large enough to impose the kind of iron-fisted bayonet rule of which the Radicals were often accused. Late in 1869, for instance, there were only 1,100 federal soldiers in all of Virginia, and just 716 in Mississippi. These were under a mandate first to keep good order, and were in fact frequently used in support of conservative whites against unruly freedmen. More irksome in practice were the state militias, which were organized by the Republican state governments and which contained substantial numbers of black men. The practice of arming blacks had dark historical resonance for whites, who had been raised to fear slave revolt above all things, and was particularly infuriating at this time. In this context, their resort to violence was not uncommon, and not without its rewards.

The first Ku Klux Klan was born at Pulaski, Tennessee, in 1865. It began as an organization of unemployed Confederates and, by the late 1860s, had become an extralegal paramilitary brotherhood,

wrapped in legendary bedsheets and shrouded in exotic ceremonies and rituals. The Klan was a radical response to what white Southerners perceived to be the attempt of the federal government radically to reorder their lives. And it prompted equally radical countermeasures. Its reputation is a curious thing. Northern liberals both then and later condemned it as an agency of racial reaction. Terror was the tool used by Klansmen. Riding on horseback to the homes of blacks and claiming to be the ghosts of Confederate soldiers, Klansmen soon resorted to deadly tools. Hangings, shootings, arson, drowning – all were inflicted by Klan members on blacks, carpetbaggers, and scalawags as the Klan began to attract more violent elements of society. Many of its original more moderate members resigned, and in 1869, General Nathan Bedford Forest ordered the Klan dissolved. Although the formal organization was ended, poor whites used Klan tactics to continue terrorizing their black neighbors into submission.

The Klan gave rise to some astounding and revolutionary legislation designed to combat it. The Ku Klux Klan Acts of 1870 and 1871 provided heavy federal penalties for interfering with any person's civil or political rights – habeas corpus could be suspended and martial law could be declared. That exercise of federal power, along with the movement's own excesses, broke the back of the first Klan, but they did not remove its causes – white resistance to radical Northern attempts to elevate black Southerners to social and political equality with white men in the South – but not in the North. Nevertheless, it was not violence that ended Reconstruction but the dogged resistance of politically sophisticated white Southerners who understood where power truly lay, and how and when to manipulate it.

They divided to rule. They knew that the Republican regimes were not seamless monoliths but uneasy coalitions of Northerners, white Southern

Above: *the interior of a slave cabin near Petersburg, Virginia. During Reconstruction, governmental reforms and constitutional amendments guaranteed blacks the right to participate in government but did little to improve their economic and social status.*

collaborators (scalawags), and blacks, held together by the perception of a common interest and the support of Northern popular opinion. In the chain of Republican control, the blacks were the weakest link, for white conservatives knew that the Radicals saved all the best plums for themselves. So the conservatives urged blacks to demand power commensurate with their numbers and to frighten and confuse their insecure patrons. At the same time they told blacks that it was they – the former planter class – who best knew the black man's needs and wants and who were truly interested in his welfare. Craven as this sounded, there was truth in it, for it was the old planter class which still held overwhelming economic power, and which did not hesitate to use it in order to control the black vote. It was the white man who still owned the land, and the

black man who was the tenant. The threat of eviction forced many blacks into voting Democratic or not voting at all. Merchants, doctors, and lawyers could and did add to the fees of politically active blacks; white employers could and did pay more for piecework done by Democratic blacks rather than by Republican ones. There were a thousand ways that the message could be brought home that certain kinds of political behavior and association carried heavy economic consequences. That threat – the threat of unemployment – in an economy still staggering from the war proved a powerful incentive for countless black men to abandon the party of Lincoln the Emancipator, just to feed their families.

White Democrats also appealed to the carpetbaggers and scalawags with invitations of forgiveness if they abandoned their cause and

Right: *three pioneers in black history. Frederick Douglass, middle, wrote* Narrative of the Life of Frederick Douglass *and published it in 1845. The account of his life as a slave fed the fires of the abolition spirit in the North. Hiram Revels, right, was the first black to hold a seat in the United States Senate. Blanche K. Bruce, left, succeeded Revels in the Senate.*

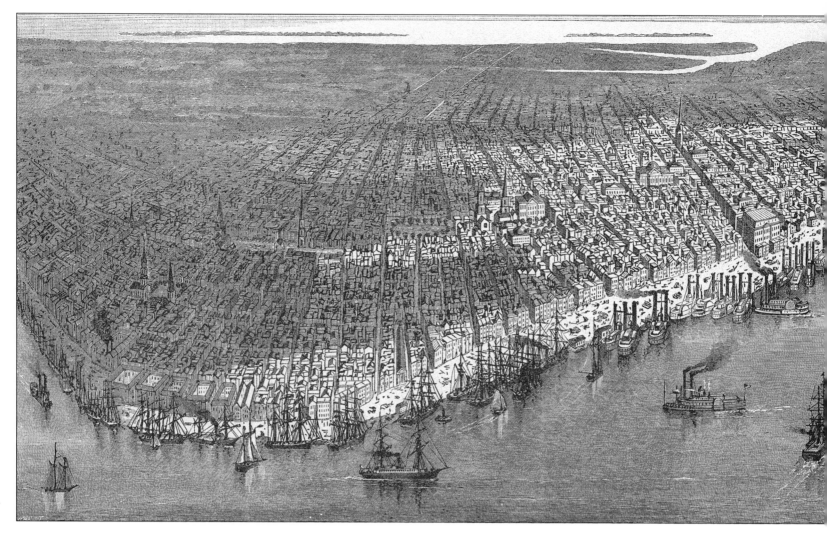

Above: *New Orleans quickly recovered from the economic devastation caused by the Civil War chiefly because of its importance as a major port and center of commerce.*

returned to the fold of white supremacy. If gentle persuasion failed, conservative whites subjected the Republicans and their supporters to an endless barrage of verbal assaults about the folly of their policies, and not just their racial policies. White landowners were told all the horror stories, some true, some invented, of how the Republicans were raising the cost of government to unbearable levels. In the antebellum period, city property had generally been taxed more heavily than farms, but under the Radical Republicans rates on agricultural land went up. Particularly vexing to Southern landowners was the knowledge that they were capital poor, and any tax at all constituted an inordinate burden and slowed down much needed investment. Government now did more for sure, but to hard-pressed farmers and planters trying to make a crop, all that mattered was that the Republican governments could be portrayed as being wasteful and extravagant with public funds. Whether their motive was to line their own pockets or to help the freedmen didn't really matter. Either from a motive was reprehensible to conservative Democrats, and both became rallying calls in their crusade to

cement white solidarity and eventually re-establish white rule.

In the end, the essence of white resistance to the Reconstruction governments came to two things: controlling the black vote and eliminating the white Republican vote, doing so in a way that would not provoke the North and that would not be declared a violation of the Fifteenth Amendment. Overt organized violence – the Klan – had failed because the nation would not tolerate so blatant a challenge from the defeated South. But means just short of violence – clearly visible community intimidation – conveyed the same unmistakable message. It was crude stuff on a mass scale: long and loud parades by armed white rifle companies; target practices using a black dummy which was then shown off in black neighborhoods; nighttime intimidation of politically active blacks; and not so gentle persuasion of their white allies to leave the South altogether and never come back.

Large themes such as "racial adjustment" always take up prominent places in the history books, and so they do in this one. But there is a danger in this.

Right: *in this illustration of the "Cotton Culture in the South" from Harper's Weekly, bales of cotton are unloaded from a steamer, workers weigh bales in the cotton yard, cotton is run through the steam press, ships are loaded with cotton at New Orleans, dealers check the quality of the cotton in a sampling room, and workers operate a bailer.*

For thousands of Southerners, the years after the Civil War were not judged by some far-off national reference points. They were a time neither of the perceived disaster of black alien rule, nor of the sparkling dawn of brotherhood and racial equality. Rather, they were years without any extraordinary moral dimension at all, when Southerners were not as preoccupied as we are commonly led to believe with either momentous political choices or intractable racial dilemmas. They were years spent trying to make a dollar, and trying to solve the immediate, local, concrete problems that come with trying to stay alive in changed and changing circumstances. The South then was a world of harvest yields, of the weather, of freight rates to market, of prices in that market, of technological change, of social resistance to change. The 1870s were hard times in the South, as elsewhere, and it was the limits of the Southern economy as much as anything else that determined that the radical reforms of Reconstruction would not succeed. In a poor region, concern for prosperity far outweighed concern for civil rights and would continue to do so until that far distant day when the South finally got to its feet.

To speak of the conditions of everyday life in the post-bellum South is to speak of agriculture, which employed the vast majority of Southern breadwinners, black and white. Throughout the period history knows as the "New South," when the region's best boosters proclaimed the urgent necessity of industrialization and the building of cities, the states of the old Confederacy remained predominantly rural. The census of 1890 reported that ninety-six percent of North Carolinians and ninety-four percent of Alabamians were not classified as "urban." Looking at the whole section, only 8.5 percent of the South was classed as urban, compared with fifty-two percent of the North Atlantic states. The numbers are important only to emphasize the fact that the conditions of life for the vast majority of Southerners were determined by the rural environment—an environment that most Americans no longer know anything about. Farming was how they made their living, and the country was where they lived. Their land, crops, and animals provided livelihood, but not only that. From their daily round they developed certain fundamental attitudes toward life, about how it should be lived, and about what the South was and should be like.

Southern agricultural trends in the late nineteenth century reflected national patterns to the extent that production expanded significantly. Southern farms

Above: *the University of Virginia in 1891. The university was founded in 1825 by Thomas Jefferson, who designed many of its buildings. By 1985, annual enrollment reached 17,400. Among its foremost alumni are Edgar Allan Poe, Woodrow Wilson, Walter Reed, and Hardy Cross Dillard.*

Above: *the promenade on the southern end of East Bay Street in Charleston, South Carolina, in 1880. Charleston and New Orleans are the two Southern cities where the influence of the French can most readily be seen. About two thousand French Huguenots moved to South Carolina between the 1680s and 1800, and most settled in or near Charleston.*

and plantations grew on a scale unknown before the war. The land was fertile, the climate warm and moist, and agricultural techniques gradually improved. And yet the benefits of great productivity seemed never to do much to improve the lot of the ordinary Southerners who spent weary lives scratching the dirt. The land prospered, but the farmer did not, and this bitterly contradicted the ancient agrarian faith, rooted so deeply in the American, and especially the Southern, psyche, that said the best life is the one lived on the soil, close to nature. That gap between what tradition said agricultural life should be and the farmers' actual experience of it led to much disillusionment and, ultimately, to a brief frenzy of political and social turmoil in the 1890s. It also led to a good deal of collective soul-searching as to what the South had become.

On the plus side, there were real reforms and improvements made in farming methods by some Southern farmers. Beginning in the 1870s, the Southern states began to establish agricultural colleges, which, by the turn of the century, they all had, and agricultural experiment stations; in addition, magazines and journals about scientific farming

provided substantial numbers of farmers with technical information on how best to rotate the crops and spread the manure. By the simplest measure all this achieved real results: production rose. Cotton remained undisputed king, though with a somewhat tarnished crown, and by 1880 yields were surpassing what they had been on the eve of the Civil War. The crop rose from 5.4 million bales in 1879 through 8.4 million in 1899 to over thirteen million in 1908. Cotton acreage also skyrocketed, partly a reflection of the westward movement of the Cotton Kingdom into Texas, which by 1900 produced thirty-four percent of the nation's crop. The older cotton states held their own, however, thanks to fertilizers that gave new life to old soil, to the preference given to cotton cultivation by the credit system, and to the force of long habit among a still largely untutored and unenterprising labor force. Tobacco, the first great staple crop and the one that had made possible the survival of Virginia back in the seventeenth century, enjoyed a remarkable comeback, spurred on by a great rise in the per capita consumption of the weed in the then dawning age of the cigarette. Rice recovered too, but did not regain its prewar prominence, while sugar – the greatest Southern cash crop after cotton – boomed. But these were the staples – the crops that Southerners had traditionally grown for sale on the world market – but they excluded a huge sector of Southern agriculture. Food crops, corn and pork especially, remained enormous though their relative importance declined. The South could feed itself, however crudely, and as rail transportation improved, it exported the abundance of its truck farms and gardens to far Northern dinner tables.

Simple abundance is easy to measure, but it must be seen in the context of the social costs and rewards it entailed. It had been the fervent hope of some Southerners who came through the Civil War that the defeat of the Old South's slaveholding class would finally lead to greater economic, as well as political, democracy in Dixie. The census of 1880 seemed to bear out their faith, when it was reported that in the cotton producing states, the numbers of farms had risen since 1860 from 449,000 to 1.1 million, and that the size of the average farm had fallen from 347 acres to 156 acres. It seemed to indicate that the day of Thomas Jefferson's happy yeoman had come at last and brought with it all the civic benefits of an enlightened and independent citizenry. To Southern poet Sydney Lanier it meant "meat and bread for which there are no notes in the bank; pigs fed with homemade corn; yarn spun, stockings knit but made and sold; eggs, chickens, products of natural animal growth, and grass at nothing a ton."

But the numbers alone were deceiving, for what had really changed in the South was the labor system and not the system of land tenure. Sharecropping had replaced slavery, and all of those alleged new farms were not in fact worked by happy Jeffersonian yeomen but by dour tenants, poor as ever and far from independent. What the sharecropper made depended less on how hard and diligently he cultivated the earth than on what the landlord – the reincarnated planter class – provided him with in terms of tools, works animals, feed, and seed. Plantation ownership had shifted from an old to a new class, who were as frequently as not urban-dwelling merchants or tradesmen. A lot of land indeed changed hands – among whites, but not from whites to blacks – but many of the big parcels were not broken up.

Sharecropping was a simple arrangement whereby the landowner decided what crops were grown and then arranged for their marketing. The proceeds were divided into thirds: one for the labor, one for the land, one for the seeds and implements. Or put another way: one-third for the cropper, two-thirds for the owner. Whatever the justice of it, it was a logical system in an economy where cash and currency were scarce and where countless

impoverished black and white agricultural workers hadn't the means to buy their own land. What happened was that the plantations once worked by gangs of slaves were divided into plots worked by tenant families – and it was each of these new units that was counted in the census as a "farm." Thus the general structure of the Old South plantation – land held in large parcels and worked by cheap labor with no other options – persisted.

Below: *an 1867 drawing by A. R. Waud of a black man voting at the polls during a state election. The Fourteenth Amendment to the Constitution denied the right of states to "abridge the privileges or immunities of citizens of the United States."*

Above: *two black children in an alley in St. Augustine, Florida. Because the Southern states were slow to ratify the Fourteenth Amendment, Congress took drastic steps to "reconstruct" the region.*

against the probable size of the crop that was the collateral, and he also decided what the interest would be. It was not unusual for the credit price for goods to be at least thirty percent above the cash price. Once a crop lien was executed between a farmer and a merchant, the farmer was effectively bound to that merchant; no others would sell him as much as a thimble, except for cash. The farmer who was unable to shop around thus found himself buying what he needed to survive in the highest possible market, but selling in the lowest market, because he had no control over when his crop was sold. That decision was up to the furnishing merchant who held the lien. It meant that at the end of the harvest, the price that a mortgaged crop brought in not uncommonly fell short of the cost of the goods advanced against it during the growing season. When that happened, a farmer was told that he had not "paid out"; that is, his crop had not paid its way. When he fell short in this way, the law then bound him to renew the lien on his next crop with the same merchant. Such a repeating mechanism doomed thousands of Southern farmers, black and white, to complete economic dependence and utterly removed the substance of their lives from the Jeffersonian ideal of the independent yeoman. If he would feed his family, the system seemed to say, a man must sacrifice his autonomy. Every mouthful his children ate put him further into debt.

From such a dismal set of facts, two questions naturally arise: who was to blame, and why didn't Southern farmers do something about it? While the crop lien system certainly offered ample opportunities for abuse on the part of the merchant, and while a few merchants actually did grind farmers as hard as they could, the merchants were not by and large the villains. They were actors in a flawed, but rational, system that had arisen out of the legitimate need for credit, when no other source of credit was available to most farmers in most parts of the South. Banks were scarce, for when the national banking laws had been rewritten in 1862, Southern agricultural interests were unrepresented in Congress. The National Banking Act that resulted was plainly biased in favor of Northern and non-agricultural interests, and the number of banks per capita in the cotton states consequently fell far below the Northern ratios. In 1894, there were 123 counties in the state of Georgia without any kind of bank.

More diversified farming would surely have helped farmers reduce their reliance on the merchants, but it would also have required transportation and marketing facilities that few parts of the rural South then had. The lien system itself worked against growing anything but cotton, which was the cash crop that the merchant himself needed to sell to his

With capital desperately short, much of Southern agriculture functioned under lien laws, which provided that a farmer could pledge to a merchant his as yet unplanted and unharvested crop in return for the loan, or simply the credit, necessary to obtain supplies needed to "make" a crop. The merchant decided the amount of supplies he would advance

Above: *Benjamin R. Tillman of South Carolina attacked the University of South Carolina as a "seedbed of the artistocracy." He and his populist followers then founded Clemson and Winthrop colleges. Although Tillman was a very wealthy man, he identified himself with the cause of small farmers.*

been burdened with the crop lien system and all the evils of sharecropping, prosperity would have proved almost impossibly elusive for small Southern farmers – and this amid the potentially most fruitful land and climate in the world.

In human terms it meant the farmer had to work harder to earn less, and if he was a tenant on a lien it meant his chances of ever throwing off the yoke of the merchant and becoming independent grew dimmer every year. As a chronic debtor, he felt most acutely the contraction of the national currency supply in a period of deflation; he contracted debts in dollars worth less than the dollars he would later have to pay back. He carried the heaviest burden of the nation's post-bellum policy of ever-rising tariffs. He was the producer of a raw material that sold on the world market at low prices, yet he purchased everything he could not raise himself from markets outside the South whose prices were inflated by protective tariffs. In the widest sense, he was mortgaged to the larger purposes of national industrialization and doomed to a position of inferiority that produced a bitter legacy with political consequences in the Populist revolt of the 1890s. But transcending politics, which were only a symptom, and the revolt, which quickly passed, it was the conditions of daily life as endured by so many Southern farmers, black and white, that declared in tragic terms that something was badly amiss in the South. Here were God's legendary "chosen people," scraping away desperately at the bottom of the pile. Perhaps reality had simply not yet caught up with the mythic expectations. Or, more likely, perhaps the new reality of post-bellum Southern agriculture was going to require some basic changes in the old myth, changes that would require factories as well as farms to secure the good life for a "New South."

The story of Southern industry in these years was a tale of how Southerners tried to construct a new myth to fit what many fervently hoped would become a new reality. It was the myth of the mighty industrialized South, which would regain for the region the wealth and national influence it could obviously never again enjoy through reliance on agriculture alone. It was an idea that fit the mood of the age, for the years after the Civil War were the time when the United States became an industrial behemoth rivaling the mightiest European states. Not even in the South was the notion of industrial revolution, or at least the notion of a balanced agricultural and industrial economy, a new one. There had been earlier, farsighted apostles of economic diversification, such as William Gregg of South Carolina, who had mounted a bold campaign to bring cotton mills to the cotton fields instead of automatically sending the cotton to the North or to

own factors and creditors. So while staple-crop production soared, it was less a symbol of genuine economic productivity than of the old Southern thralldom to a few cash crops. The merchants were classic, and classically abused, middlemen who generally charged high rates because they themselves took enormous risks. They were betting on the behavior of human beings and on the cooperation of the weather, and their prices had to account for any number of total failures among those whose liens they held.

The Southern farmer also labored under disadvantages that were not unique to the South but were shared with farmers elsewhere, especially in the West. The late nineteenth century was a time of falling prices, and those of the great staple crops were no exception. So serious was the decline that, for example, the cotton crop of 1873 of something over nine million bales raised more in the market than the crop of 1894 which came in at almost twenty-four million bales. The South was tied into world-wide agricultural depression, and even had it not

Above: *Louisville, Kentucky, in 1872. Founded in 1778, Louisville is located at the falls of the Ohio River. After the Civil War, the city, known as "The Gateway to the South," was an important manufacturing center. Among its products were alcoholic beverages, meat, farm implements, tobacco, and wooden goods.*

Europe. But now, in the wake of Reconstruction, when the missionary spirit of the nation had been aroused to reform the backward South toward more enlightened political behavior and racial attitudes, a new zeal was also kindled on behalf of the less controversial, but equally difficult to achieve, goal of economic expansion and diversification. Thousands of Northerners had come to realize that the underdeveloped South presented vast opportunities. It offered ingredients of early-stage industrial development in abundance: land, timber, coal, water power, and cheap labor. "How to get rich in the South" propaganda streamed out of the North, and countless after-dinner speeches to eager groups of Northern businessmen and investors began with ringing admonitions to "Go South, Young Man ... ."

Many Southerners, eager to put away the rancor of the war and Reconstruction, seemed keen to embrace their share of the nation's new industrial destiny. In a spirit of sectional reconciliation undergirded by a common desire for profits and prosperity, they welcomed the Yankee investors and industrialists and not just with words. Pliant, conservative-dominated Southern legislatures got in the habit of never saying "no" to anyone and of granting liberal concessions to anybody with capital

and a plan for doing something with it in their part of the world. Vast tracts of mineral and timber lands were opened to private development. Railroad construction followed apace, giving access to many of the landlocked parts of Dixie; and scores of small lines were swallowed up into larger systems. Fittingly, it was the railroads that provided probably the most vivid example of the South's desire to conform, economically at least, to the standards of the old Northern enemy. The gauge of Southern railroad tracks had always differed from Northern lines by three inches. So, on May 30, 1886, after meticulous preparations, the Louisville & Nashville Railroad, one of the South's largest, put 8,000 men to work moving the west rail three inches east along 2,000 miles of track and adjusting the wheels on 300 locomotives and 10,000 railroad cars.

With expanding railroads, much the most magical technology of the age, the way was opened for the development of the South's vast iron ore and coal deposits and for the weed-like growth of cities such as Birmingham, Alabama, which Southerners John T. Milner and Daniel Pratt did their best, quite successfully, to turn into the Pittsburgh of the South. By 1898, Birmingham had become the largest source of pig iron in the United States and the third largest source in the whole world – yet, in 1860, there had been nothing there at all. Beginning in the middle and late 1880s, the South's oldest cash crop, tobacco, proved that it too offered new market opportunities. In antebellum times, the processing of tobacco, once the crop left the field, had been largely a handicraft-type operation. By the turn of the century the production of chewing and smoking tobacco products had been thoroughly mechanized, the demand spurred on by new fashions in smoking that favored

Carolina-grown bright leaf suitable for that genteel new smoke, the cigarette. It was the revitalized tobacco business that occasioned the conspicuous rise of one of the New South's most famous families. In 1869, with two blind mules and a wagon-load of tobacco, James Buchanan Duke began his long rise to the top of the firm that, by 1889, would produce one half of all the cigarettes smoked in America, and that, a year later, would absorb most of its competitors to become the mammoth American Tobacco

Left: *a cartoon depicts the fickle "Miss Textile Industries" directing her attentions not to New England, where the majority of textile mills had been located, but to the New South, where fuel and labor costs were cheaper.*

Above: *An 1867 drawing from* Harper's Weekly *shows Southern agricultural workers harvesting crops from "historic fields" where a Civil War battle had taken place only a few years before.*

Company. Duke was especially skilled and lucky, as the size of his fortune proved, but in achieving such success in the wide-open field of Southern industrialization, he was certainly not alone.

Without question, however, the greatest substance and the greatest symbolism of the new industrializing South grew from the crop most closely identified with the region: cotton. More than anything else, the cotton mill came to typify the effort of the South to be like the North. Between 1880 and 1900, the number of Southern mills rose from 161 to some 400, which

far outstripped the rest of the country. The motives behind it all were varied, and profit was primary for sure. But the cotton mill crusade, more than other forms of economic diversification, did manage to transpose a simple drive for development into genuine community enthusiasm for the social as well as the material benefits that the mills allegedly brought with them. Chamber of commerce newspapers once again took up the gospel of bringing the factories to the fields as the best way to rehabilitate the region. But while much of the initial capitalization came from local Southern sources, absentee ownership increased and so deflated whatever philanthropic impact the mills might once have had in bringing employment and better lives to thousands of Southern farmers who flocked, with their families, to take jobs as operatives ("lintheads" as they soon became known) in scores of Southern milltowns.

Viewed on the surface, the South's industrial progress seemed impressive, and yet it was still tarnished not far below. True, the South advanced, but so did the rest of the nation, so much so in fact that in the thirty-five years after the Civil War the states of the old Confederacy actually lost relative ground and ended up with a smaller percentage of the nation's factories than before the war. In addition to merely counting the numbers of factories, it is important to note what kind of factories they were. This first big-time Southern brush with industrialization brought largely low-grade and low-wage industries of the kind that gave the first and the roughest processing to raw materials. These were industries closely tied to agriculture, forestry, and mining. The South's industrial output in these years consisted of things such as cotton yarn, coarse cloth, cane sugar, turpentine, liquor, board lumber, and tobacco products. Theirs were industries that, per wage earner, added only small value to a product. The finished cotton and lumber products that reached world consumers were not necessarily cheap, but they were cheaply produced in the South in the initial stages. The region had induced capital and manufacturing to come to it by offering everything at its command more cheaply – taxes, power, land, raw materials, and especially labor. But once the initial processing had been done in the South, the final, more valuable work was done somewhere else. The great furniture industry that developed in North Carolina was the only major exception to this rule.

Like Southern agriculture, Southern industry was fundamentally extractive, and because of this, the South's relationship with the North remained fundamentally colonial. In 1910, sixty-two percent of all Southern workers were producing raw materials and, as is characteristic of raw material economies, most of them earned low wages and had little prospect of ever doing anything else in those industries. The South was saddled with such arrangements not out of any Yankee conspiracy to keep it subordinate, though that was one consequence, but because of a whole complex of issues, some chargeable to the South itself. It is true that Northern-controlled railroads discriminated in the structure of their freight rates and that price differentials were imposed on Birmingham-produced steel. But there were other obstacles as well to what might have been a better-balanced development: the late start, the lack of local capital and of a skilled labor force, and the tug of an ancient agrarian tradition that warned darkly that industrialization might not be the best way to proceed.

However, the greatest obstacle was probably the new configuration of political and economic power that had resulted from the Civil War and the painful process of reunion. The outcome was a gross sectional imbalance, in favor of the Northeast over both the South and the West. The Northeast had become an imperial power within the nation, and its program of neo-mercantilism, reminiscent of the eighteenth century, flowed naturally from the new alignment of forces. As the established workshop of the nation, the North discouraged the development of competition elsewhere while promoting the production and crude finishing of the raw materials that fed its own factories. Like imperial Britain, then also reaching its zenith, the Northeast controlled the freight trade through the structure of railroad rates. If industrial production can be said to have four stages – extraction, processing, transportation, and distribution – then in late nineteenth-century America the final three were reserved for the Northeast. The first, and the lowest profit-producing or the four, was left to the poor South, which contributed at the lowest, most basic and cheapest level to the great engine of industrial power that the American economy had become.

Unequal though the system certainly was, it had, even so, benefits not dreamed of earlier. So it was that rational Southern businessmen and conservative politicians sang its praises with loud and united voice through their policies of tax exemptions and grants and subsidies to keep the ball rolling merrily along. The economic, social, and human costs they

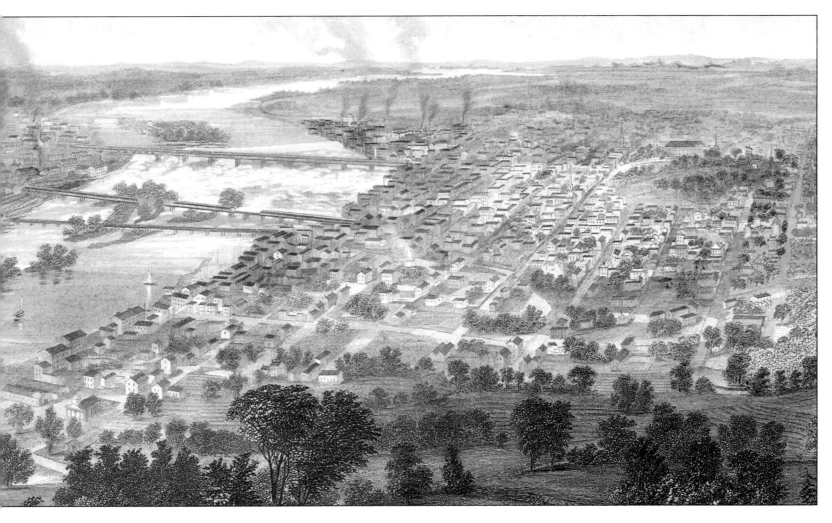

Above: *a view of Richmond, Virginia, in 1868 shows the James River, the James River Canal, and the iron and flour mills. Increasingly, the city turned to manufacturing for its livelihood.*

Left: *agricultural workers tend the tobacco crop. The first consumption of tobacco was by pipe smoking. By the mid-eighteenth century, snuff became popular. The nineteenth century ushered in the era of chewing tobacco, cigar, and cigarette.*

wrote off to progress, or the hope of it; and the costs of this kind of primitive industrialization could be considerable, as the regional comparison suggested. In terms of general living standards, wealth and welfare, the South was as separated from the rest of the Union as it had been in 1850. Its per capita income in 1880 was $376, compared with $870 in the North; in 1900, this had risen to $509 in the South and $1,165 in the North; in 1912, the South's per capita income was $993, the North's $1,950. By 1920, the eleven American states with the lowest per capita income were all Southern, with Alabama at the bottom and Louisiana at the top. Thus poverty joined with race, religion, and the memory of defeat to set the South apart as America's most sectional of sections.

The deeply ambiguous nature of Southern economic conditions in the late nineteenth and early twentieth centuries, and the stunted performance that resulted, should be measured by past, not future, standards. The South then was clearly not the sort of place that most Southerners today, black or white, would like to imagine themselves living in. But neither were those businessmen, promoters, and planters – along with their Northern partners – being utterly cynical in selling precious things seemingly cheap and opening the South to changes whose profits and perils no man could then perfectly foresee. It is easy now to judge them harshly for their benighted racial attitudes and insensitivity to the welfare of their society's lower orders. But these are relative things, and by the standards of the age itself, when all the world was racist and few farmers or workers anywhere had an easy time of it, their actions were neither ignoble in motive nor cataclysmic in consequence. On the other hand their suspicions about the intrusive nature of the state, and their pronounced convictions about its limited ability to do good and its less limited ability to do evil, have had distinct echoes in more modern times. Their legacy to the more modern South, the South which would ultimately exorcise the devil of race but would still remain caught between tradition and change on so many other matters, is as powerful as any legacy left by either the masters or the slaves of antebellum times. It is also perhaps a more instructive legacy for Southerners today, who are as determined as ever to be Southern, but rich and American too.

6

THE ENDURING SECTION

O ut of the hard circumstances of post-bellum Southern life came one fundamental theme that endured far into the twentieth century. The exhilaration and the devastation of the Civil War, the radical social and political experimentation of Reconstruction, and the travail of the post-slavery cotton economy made the region and the people who lived there unusually conscious of the competing claims of continuity and change. Southerners white and black were a people whose engrained cultural habits reached back to a time – the antebellum era – that was in many ways at war with the modern world. The Civil War or, as Southerners always preferred to call it, the War of Southern Independence brought the old ways to a shattering end. The remaining years of the nineteenth century presented, in their glimpses of an alternative racial order and in their flirtation with industrialism, possibilities that it would take much of the twentieth century to bring fully to life. When that finally happened, Southerners found themselves more closely integrated into the life of the nation than at any time since the founding of the Republic, yet they were regretful for the worlds they had lost en route. To understand their journey to the many new Souths of the twentieth century, it is helpful to consider more closely their historical point of departure.

The centerpiece and most lasting symbol of that first new South – the cotton mill crusade – bespoke a determined effort to transform and uplift the material conditions of life in the South, but behind it and related reforms was a stronger drive to alter the South's spirit as well. Much of Southern history in the twentieth century – a war of the mind and spirit between the contending forces of tradition and change

Left: *the Chamber of Commerce building in Charleston, South Carolina. Organized in 1773, the chamber is the oldest such organization in America.*

– springs from these early skirmishes. When, in New York City, on December 21, 1886, Atlanta newspaperman Henry W. Grady delivered an address entitled "The New South," he fathered a movement that long outlived him and that future generations each in their turn and in their own way would call "new." Grady had in mind the economic rejuvenation of his native region. To achieve it, he seemed willing to sell his soul to the industrialists and entrepreneurs in his audience. The time had come to put away sectional animosity and to forget the rancor of war and its aftermath; only if old suspicions and fears were allayed could the North be persuaded to give of her talents and resources to resuscitate the South's economy. The South must, he said, have Northern know-how, Northern money, and Northern ideas if she were ever to break out of the poverty and powerlessness that had oppressed her since 1865.

All those New York industrialists whom Grady invited down to Dixie, enthusiastic as they plainly were, did not dispense their favors free of charge. The economic price they exacted, and that Southerners such as Grady agreed to pay, has been much remarked on as imprisoning the South in a self-defeating "colonial economy": Southern enterprises controlled from Northern boardrooms; Southern factories feeding the profits of Northern shareholders. A second, and to some more insidious, price was paid when the South accepted Northern business methods along with Northern capital. Out-Yankee the Yankee, Grady seemed to say. Whatever had been the attitudes and values of the industrialists who had made North into the great and rich power she was, and who had done so much to raise the standard of living of her people, must then be the best values for the South too. From among countless Southerners tired simply of being poor, Grady and his spiritual heirs found ample, talented converts. The problem with the South, according to these tireless apostles of change, was that there had always been too many dawdling, usually slaveholding, old gentlemen, and not nearly enough hard-headed businessmen with both the money to invest in something besides land and slaves and the common sense to put economic development ahead of sentimental old traditions. They stood for progress, by which they meant that no reasonable man could doubt for a moment that the future would be infinitely better than the past, and that material prosperity was the primary goal toward which Southerners' energies and ambitions should be directed.

Integral to the South's economic reformation was the South's intellectual reformation, according to Grady's spiritual kinsman, Walter Hines Page. Page spent the better part of his career trying to persuade the Southern states to establish and then support a

system of public schools in which ambitious Southern youths could get all the training they needed to secure places in the new industrial order. To symbolize his particular crusade, Page conjured an image of "The Forgotten Man" of the South, whose degraded status Page blamed on the allegedly aristocrat-ridden, undemocratic heritage of the antebellum era. Page had much of his history wrong, but it was the interpretation that mattered, for his was an interpretation that provided someone to blame – much as Grady had blamed the planters for the South's stymied industrial performance. Even so, Page dwelt upon the future and not the past, and what he hoped to see – if Southerners could discard the bad habits of their ancestors – was sound practical education in the basic intellectual skills, and vocational training tailored to the needs of developing Southern industry. The Latin, Greek, theology, and moral philosophy of the private academies of the Old South had to go, and once they had the way would be clear to meet the needs of the little man, who, with a decent education, would never again let himself come under the domination of a small class of aristocrats. With the burden of ignorance lifted from his shoulders and in possession of the skills demanded by modern society, the common man of the New South would never again let himself be forgotten by anyone. Page's model, like Grady's, lay in the North, whose experience with free public education he held up as the inevitable course of the

Left: *American orator Henry Woodfin Grady coined the phrase, "The New South," in an 1886 speech in New York City. He called for an economic rejuvenation of the region and attempted to persuade Northern industrialists to move their companies to the South.*

future. As if overnight, Massachusetts, the seedbed of radical anti-Southern abolitionism, was put aside for Massachusetts, the home of Horace Mann and free schools for all.

To Page, and his ilk of Southern progressive for years to come, the free public school became both a panacea – as the factory was for Grady – for all that ailed the South and the vehicle that would redeem all the dead weight of its benighted past. It was offered as a tonic guaranteed to strengthen democracy by giving to "everyman" the equipment he needed

to prove himself equal to every other man, and rising generations of Southerners were to be fitted out with a new kind of instrumental knowledge that was vastly superior to any of the old. With such an education, a man might look forward to a future as bright as he himself chose to make it.

There was about all of this an unmistakable dawn-world optimism that what men wanted to do they could do, and that what they could do would bring happiness to them and their children. This was a conviction widely shared throughout the western

Below: *a farmer plows his cotton fields in South Carolina. Even with an influx of industry and business, the South remained primarily rural in character.*

world at the beginning of the twentieth century, and it is no surprise that Southerners should desire to partake of it. Southerners had always been Americans too, and it was America that then led the world in what seemed the steady and irreversible march of progress. The world was at peace; it was developing its human and natural resources; and it was becoming rich beyond the imagining of earlier generations. The New South, as it was first conceived and ever after elaborated, fitted comfortably within this mainstream. The South had of course to start from a lower point than the rest of America, and it seemed that Southerners always had to run harder just to keep up. But about the worthiness of the race itself, prophets of the New South had no doubts. So spacious was their faith that there was even room in it for the South's most forgotten man, the black.

It was room of a qualified sort that would in fact later embarrass more modern "new" Southerners, but that by the standards of an earlier age was neither malicious in design nor completely ill-advised in result. By accommodating black Southerners, however modestly, within their planned new South, the advocates of change hoped fervently, and in sincere good faith, that they could settle the race question at least for their lifetimes. By and large, they did. In this, they were helped by an astounding black man whose fate, sadly, at the hands of later generations of black and white men has not been a particularly happy one.

Booker T. Washington, born a slave, became the greatest black spokesman that the New South produced. Washington saw with equal clarity the degraded condition of life for the vast majority of blacks and the immovable object of virulent race prejudice that then held nearly all of white America captive. At the same time, he heard all the grand promises of the New South and saw the gains in material prosperity that the movement seemed to be making. From this, he concluded that no sane white man who truly hoped for the progress of his section could profit in any way by keeping millions of blacks in a condition of perpetual serfdom. It went against the grain of New South practicality not to admit everyone to the bandwagon, even though it went without saying that black Southerners would only ride at the rear. But riding at the rear was better than not at all, and it was, Washington understood, about the best that could be expected. So he put forward his famous program for the vocational education of

Right: *the Old South romanticized in a 1908 painting by E. L. Henry. The myth of the Old South, where living was easy and manners were courtly, remained a powerful image.*

blacks both in skills that would enable them to support themselves and their families in modest comfort and in trades that would give them some claim to the prosperity brought about by wider economic changes. Washington's enduring monument was Tuskegee Institute in Alabama, an industrial training center where he hoped to educate blacks in the most practical ways of being useful to their own community.

But Washington is also especially remembered for the words that perhaps most fully captured his understanding of the role blacks should play in the South of his day. Speaking at the Atlanta Cotton States and International Exposition in 1895, he pronounced what became known as his "Atlanta Compromise," and in it he asked blacks to forgo the then unattainable dream of social equality and to pursue such economic and educational goals as the South actually offered. He was roundly reviled by more radical advocates of equality, notably W. E. Burghardt Du Bois, who would become editor of *The Crisis*, the publication of the National Association for the Advancement of Colored People. But it was Washington, and not those on his left, who best understood the mood of the times; he said it was more essential for a black to be able to earn a dollar at a good job than to be able to spend a dollar in the same opera house as a white man.

Today, Washington's measures seem mild, halfhearted, and to some even "Uncle Tomish." Then, however, they seemed prudent and not without a genuine vision for the black race. Just a year after Washington's Atlanta Compromise address, in the case of *Plessy v. Ferguson*, the United States Supreme Court effectively scotched any notions of black social equality with its famous doctrine of "separate but equal." Racial segregation in public accommodation and education, the court said, could not be construed as "unequal" or as "discriminatory" so long as the facilities available to both races were comparable in quality. Even though things in the South were, in fact, almost always separate but unequal, "separate but equal" remained the law of the land for race relations in all of America until the 1950s. And in the South, which was where the vast majority of blacks still lived, a rigorous pattern of social segregation – the era of Jim Crow – clamped down on the black with unrelenting discipline.

About the New South's promises of industrial power, intellectual rejuvenation and racial harmony there was wide, but hardly universal, agreement. The New South preached a gospel of change in a land where old habits died slowly and where the agrarian tradition continued to grip thousands of Southerners with awesome tenacity. It was the gap that existed between the sort of future the New

South promised and the conditions of rural life as actually experienced by the majority of Southerners that fueled the Populist upheavals of the 1890s. Then, in the context of a world-wide depression more severe than anything Americans had yet experienced, Southern and Western farmers momentarily united to do battle against their perceived oppressors: the banks, the railroads, the trusts, the tariff, and the ruling conservative spokesmen for these things. In the South, where the roots of the agrarian heritage went deepest and where the disjuncture between the myth and the reality of rural life seemed most severe, Populism (as the movement and the party came to be known) took on its most virulent cast. The farmers organized themselves first through the Granges, then through the Farmers' Alliances, and finally into the Populist Party. Grouped behind fiery leaders such as Tom Watson of Georgia, "Pitchfork" Benjamin Tillman of South Carolina, and Stephen Hogg of Texas, they loudly asserted their dissent from the claims of the New South. The Farmers' Alliance, founded in 1875 in Texas, was vocal in protesting land monopolies at state level. The movement spread to other Southern states, as did the Agricultural Wheel, formed initially in Arkansas. By 1890, the combined Alliance, Wheel, and Farmers' Union claimed more than two million members. Their success in politics was fleeting, and while they fielded their own third-party presidential candidate in the election of 1892, their "fusion" with the Democrats four years later and the subsequent defeat of Democratic candidate William Jennings Bryan by Ohio Republican William McKinley, spelled the doom of organized agrarian political revolt. But the sense of grievance that had given it life – the grievance of the small farmers of the South who were left out of the New South's vision of a brighter tomorrow – did not vanish with the Populist Party.

Above: *a view of Broad Street, in Charleston's financial district.*

Left: *members of a black family pose on the porch of their cabin in Florida. At the turn of the century, the contrast between the economic levels of average black families and white ones was sharp, and was to linger over the next several decades.*

Voting rights were denied to huge numbers of blacks and small farmers when the Southern states amended their constitutions to include poll taxes, residency requirements, and literacy tests, called the "understanding clause" or the "Mississippi Plan." In Mississippi, the new voting requirements reduced the size of the electorate from 250,000 to 77,000. And throughout the South, the Democratic Party remained solidly in power.

The first years of the new century seemed to confirm that Populism was but an interlude on the happy road to the progress the New South had prescribed. In 1898, the United States involved itself in the Spanish-American War, a conflict that finished off European colonial power in the New World and that witnessed a resurgence of national patriotism to which the South was not immune. Southerners flocked to the colors, much as they had in 1861. Veterans of the Civil War, including Fitzhugh Lee and "Fighting Joe" Wheeler, served as Major Generals, and sons of Confederate veterans donned blue uniforms and joined with their Northern counterparts in the conflict. As Populist Ben Tillman put it: "Populists, Democrats, Republicans are we, but we're all American to make Cuba free." After the election of 1896, the whole country had veered to the right under Republican leadership, and the conservative Democratic leaders of the Southern states happily fell into line. The South shared in the spirit of the larger national life in other ways too. As had been the case with Populism, when Southern farmers found themselves allied with comrades in the West, the Progressive movement of the years leading up to World War I also penetrated the South, adding a new dimension to the future new Southerners said they wanted to build. Nationally, the names of Theodore Roosevelt, Woodrow Wilson, and Robert La Folette symbolized the movement, but they had Southern accomplices. If there was one main theme to Progressivism, it was the determination to break the web of economic privilege that had come to entangle the life of the nation during half a century of industrialization. Progressives launched vigorous attacks on what they liked to term "the interests" – a catch-all label for anyone suspected of monopolizing the benefits of a bountiful economy – and they proposed myriad regulatory antidotes to the pernicious influence of the trusts, the corporations, and the railroads. They produced an impressive array of legislation and executive policy at local, state, and federal levels. Gas and water socialism, the Northern Securities Case, the Hepburn Act, pure food laws, commission government, the Federal Reserve System, the income tax, and a commerce department all reflected the broad range of the Progressive impulse. In the battle against "the

The Populist interlude highlighted an unmistakable fact of Southern political life. To white voters, Populism spelled a split in the Democratic South, a split that could easily result in political control by blacks.

The purchasing of black votes had been common on both sides in the 1892 election and earlier. Populists farmers sought the votes of blacks in order to defeat the Bourbons; Democratic Bourbons sought the votes of blacks to maintain political control. As election fraud came to light, Henry Cabot Lodge proposed a "Force Bill," to provide federal supervision of national elections. The measure passed in the House but was defeated in the Senate. Despite its defeat, the bill hinted at trouble to come. The Southern Bourbons took action to disfranchise blacks and small white farmers, thus ensuring continued political control.

Above: *Booker T. Washington, born a slave in Virginia, founded Tuskegee Institute in Alabama in order to provide much-needed vocational training to black Americans.*

Above right: *W. E. B. DuBois, educator and writer, was the first black to receive a Ph.D. from Harvard University. After the 1909 founding of the National Association for the Advancement of Colored People (NAACP), DuBois served as an officer of the organization and edited its journal entitled* The Crisis.

interests," it was the Progressive instinct that public, not private, action held the greatest promise for reform – an instinct that, especially in the South, encountered old suspicions about the dangers of centralized political power.

Some Progressives were men tied to the older experience of agrarian protest. Others were old-fashioned moral reformers determined to destroy materialism, but not private property, through their own well-developed sense of public duty, responsibility, and character. Still others belonged to the nation's rising middle class, whose sense of identity and interest inhered in their professions: lawyers, doctors, and businessmen with new management expertise. Southern Progressives generally fell into these national patterns, but they also possessed certain characteristics in keeping with the region's past. While Southern Progressives did not share Populism's overwhelmingly rural cast, they did share the old Southern inclination to seek out an outside enemy to blame for the region's ills, and in the banks, the utility companies and the

railroads they found just such an enemy. The ranks of the Southern Progressives included a vivid array of characters. Napoleon P. Broward, who had led the rough-and-tumble life as a deckhand at sea, was elected governor of Florida in 1904 and became the champion of the little man against the railroads, the timber barons, and the land pirates that Florida was full of. William Goebel, son of German immigrants, led the struggle in Kentucky for railroad regulation and corporate taxation. In Alabama, millionaire Birmingham businessman Braxton Bragg Comer took on the mighty Louisville & Nashville Railroad. In Georgia, Hoke Smith led the Progressive battle in coalition with the old agrarian radical Tom Watson. North Carolinian Charles B. Aycock became a great apostle of education. James K. Vardaman, who wore long hair and a tailcoat and campaigned from a lumber wagon pulled by oxen, was elected governor of Mississippi in 1903. An absolute reactionary in racial matters, he was nevertheless a Progressive in matters of social and economic reform. On the comic fringe, Arkansan Jeff Davis, who served as both a

governor and a United States senator, pitted the rednecks against the "high-collared roosters" and earned the sobriquet "Karl Marx of the Hillbillies."

The accomplishments of these men and others like them were not inconsiderable. A system of direct primary elections had been established in a majority of Southern states by 1903 and in all of them by 1915. Demand for primary election reform was especially strong, since in the one-party, Solid South nomination was tantamount to election. At the same time it is important to remember that the primaries in the South were exclusively white primaries that did nothing to advance the political rights of utterly disenfranchised blacks. State commissions were established to regulate the public utilities and the railroads. Safety inspections began in mines and factories; prison reform was at least put in motion. Southern anti-trust laws of the Progressive era suggested, mistakenly, that monopolies had gone for good. North Carolina boldly attacked the practices of the tobacco trust, and in Kentucky and Tennessee hostility spilled over into actual violence in the

Above: *Booker T. Washington (seated in front on the left) and some of his associates at the Tuskegee Institute. Washington was appalled by the state of education for blacks. In 1910, high-school enrollment for blacks totaled only 8,000 in the entire South. Despite his efforts to change that state of affairs, around this time many blacks turned away from Washington toward the more aggressive W. E. B. DuBois, who urged blacks to reject their status as second-class citizens.*

"Black Patch Tobacco Wars" of 1907 and 1908. In Southern cities, commission and city manager forms of municipal government made notable advances. On Progressivism's parochial side, prohibition made even more notable advances. Local option by county became the rule, and even in Kentucky, the home of bourbon whiskey, ninety-four out of 119 counties were dry by 1908. Pinched and ill-advised as it may have been, prohibition grew up naturally among the almost totally native-born Protestant population of the rural South, and it remained a fighting cause in rural areas long after the urban South had embraced the cocktail lounge and the liquor store.

International conflicts have a way of intruding onto the domestic scene, and World War I was no exception. More than anything, unless it was outside interference in racial matters, Southerners feared the disruption of world trade and with it that of their export markets for cotton. With the outbreak of hostilities in Europe in 1914, key cotton exchanges did not open, and prices initially tumbled. While Allied demand had driven prices back to record peaks by the end of the war, the message was that the South, as ever, was subject to outside events and was compelled to react to them. At this stage, some spokesmen even proposed state financing for cotton warehouses as a means of helping farmers wait for better prices, and thus, in the urgency of the moment, threw their laissez-faire scruples to the wind. The war forced Southerners, as it did other Americans, to take a stand and to look outward generally. With its heavily Anglo-Saxon population, the South was staunchly pro-Ally from beginning to end, and when the call to the American colors finally came in 1917 and 1918, the old Southern spirit showed itself. While there was some progressive suspicion of militarism and dark talk about the profits made by munitions' manufacturers, Southerners generally responded as if it had been 1861. But whereas during the Civil War, Southerners had jealously resisted the centralizing efforts of their own Confederate government in Richmond, in this war Southern congressmen, in the name of national security, largely acquiesced in a wide array of sweeping federal legislation brought on by the war. This included the Railroad Act, which placed the railroads under federal authority for the duration, new alien and sedition acts, increases in the Progressive federal income tax, and national conscription. A million Southerners served, and while not all got the chance they wanted to fight the Germans in France, they at least got the chance to mingle with recruits from other parts of their own country. Experiences were shared, and differences were muffled in the emotion of patriotism. Due both to its congressional influence and to its felicitous climate that made year-round training possible, military camps and bases proliferated in the South, and many continued on in peacetime. A Southern port, Norfolk / Hampton / Newport News, in Virginia, became an important embarkation point and home to an ever more immense American fleet. The wartime boom – once the initial cotton panic had passed – gave fresh substance to the New South's now no longer so new boasts that industrialization was the sure path to a prosperous future. Munitions factories in Tennessee and Virginia, chemical plants in Alabama, and textile mills all over the region pulled Southerners out of the fields and, in what was a new experience for many, gave them a taste of earning real money.

When the war ended with an Allied victory made possible by American intervention, the whole nation dashed toward the 1920s with pent-up energy. The industrial boom started by the war expanded and, in the water-power-rich South, this boom was increasingly driven by the magic of a new age: electricity. The chemical and textile industries especially profited from electrification, and the region of the Carolina Piedmont overtook New England as the nation's primary consumer of the South's raw cotton. The fashion for cigarettes and an increasing number of female smokers gave new life to the South's oldest source of wealth, tobacco, and it was at this time that names such as "Camel," "Chesterfield," "Lucky Strike," and "Old Golds" entered the American vernacular. But none of these could match, for lasting totem-like status, the Southern beverage that had first been brewed by an Atlanta druggist in 1886 and then made famous – and fabulously profitable – by Atlantan Robert Woodruff in the 1920s: Coca-Cola.

Timber, a more natural Southern growth crop, was felled from the region's pine and hardwood forests to feed both the decade's national building boom and the South's own furniture factories and paper mills. Birmingham continued to produce iron and steel, although it was handicapped by Northern ownership that discriminated in favor of Pittsburgh mills. A petrochemical industry sprang from the wartime munitions business, as old powder plants in Tennessee and Virginia were converted to the production of cellulose-based rayon. And though it is usually thought of chiefly in connection with the West, the petroleum industry reared its head in the South too, to become both a burden and blessing for years to come. Wells in Texas fed the hunger for gasoline, sparked by the first automobiles, and refineries changed the shape of the Louisiana coastline and the banks of the Mississippi River from New Orleans to Baton Rouge.

Such development happened thanks to the active connivance between Northern and Southern boosters.

As their fathers before them in the first "new" South of the 1880s, Southerners were not to be outdone in promoting the allegedly salvific nature of industrialization. No state government was without its departments of commerce, immigration, publicity, advertising, and "progress." No small-town booster failed to believe that his town could also become the next metropolitan success story. But while every county seat had its pretensions, the city of Atlanta, which Sherman had burned to the ground in 1864 but which rose so famously from its own ashes, best symbolized the twenties' crazy mix of glitter and solid economic substance. Today, Atlanta's airport is the busiest in America; then, its railroad stations posted arrivals and departures for 150 passenger trains every day. Hundreds of conventions attracted tens of thousands of visitors. There were office skyscrapers, the luxurious Biltmore Hotel, schools

Above: *George Washington Carver (1864-1943), a noted American botanist. Educated at Iowa State, Carver went on to teach others about the importance of soil improvement and conservation.*

Facing page: *students work on soil analysis in the laboratory operated by George Washington Carver, director of agricultural studies at the Tuskegee Institute in Alamaba until his death in 1943.*

and colleges, a home-grown symphony orchestra, and a yearly visit by the Metropolitan Opera. Farther to the South, the Florida Boom exhibited all the glitter with rather less substance. Miami, Tampa, St. Petersburg, and Jacksonville mushroomed; Coral Gables, "an American Venice" and the inspiration of local fruit grower and realtor George Merrick, was invented. It took the great hurricane of 1926 finally to end the binge.

However, neither natural disaster nor man-made panic, it seemed, could dampen for long the exuberance that characterized the twenties throughout the South. "There is a thrill in the air," commented one visitor in 1927. "Big tomorrows seem to be coming around the corner. Everywhere are new roads, new automobiles, new hot dog stands, tea shops, movie palaces, radio stores, real estate subdivisions, tourist camp grounds." In 1929, the year of the Great Crash that did finally put an end to much of it, Virginia Governor Harry F. Byrd perhaps captured the spirit best, when he likened the South's current experience to the exhilaration that attended the exploitation of other, older American frontiers: "The South is being pointed to today as the West was in a former period – as the land of promise."

The "promise," however, was better kept in some respects than in others. As clearly as the change seemed to be written into the triumphant New South of the 1920s, there were still many Southerners who were reluctant or unable to read the message. Change could frighten as well as entice, and if one checked the balance at the end of the decade, continuity still counted for much in the South. Hesitation about change was not exclusive to the South: it was, for example, in the 1920s that restrictive national immigration laws were enacted to preserve the Anglo-Saxon character of America. Antisemitism, anti-Catholicism, and of course anti-black feeling rose to new heights among the nation's and the region's less enlightened folk. The popularity of D. W. Griffith's early (1915) film classic, *The Birth of a Nation*, which was based on Thomas Dixon's novel *The Clansman*, was a barometer of such feeling. Dixon was from North Carolina and Griffith from Kentucky, and the film took merciless revenge on the evils – seen from the white point of view – of Radical Reconstruction. At the end, black militiamen are put to flight by heroic Ku Klux Klansmen – the rebirth of whom soon spread that movement's own brand of bigotry across the South. The Klan, which was reborn on Stone Mountain in Georgia on Thanksgiving night, 1915, is famous for its odd rituals, preposterous titles, and flowing white robes, and it still skulks about the South today, representing the anachronistic voice of white supremacy. Then, it was the authentic voice not only of the South's unrelenting race

prejudice but also of the more general anxiety among a rural people that change was making a shambles of old moral certainties. In this respect, the Klan did not mirror only Southern anxiety, and indeed some of its greatest "successes" came from far afield, particularly from Indiana where it actually operated a successful political machine.

But the Klan's general lack of a well-articulated program bespoke its truer nature – that of the defense mechanism, and death rattle, of a dying America and a more slowly dying South. The Klan spoke for a return to respect for white womanhood and against the new moral laxness epitomized by the twenties "flapper" generation; it railed against liberalism in schools and colleges and called on the churches to gather in the wayward and return their flocks to the old-time religion. The movement warned against the dangerous influence of Jews, Catholics, and foreigners, and of course it stood for the absolute

Above: *Republican William McKinley of Ohio won the presidential elections of 1896 and 1900. During his administrations, a wave of progressivism, aimed at controlling governmental corruption, regulating big business, and reforming social conditions, swept through the country.*

Right: *Theodore Roosevelt became president in September 1901 when McKinley was assassinated. At forty-two, Roosevelt was the youngest president up to that time.*

domination of black Southerners by white ones, no matter how lowly those whites happened to be. Indeed, much of the Klan was lowly enough, its sociology reflecting that of much of the South's rural population. For such ill-educated people, whose daily lives were an endless (and for many hopeless) routine of planting and waiting for the cotton to grow, the rituals and mystique of the hooded order fostered a sense of camaraderie and belonging amid the distress of an otherwise grim agricultural existence. The price of admission was ten dollars, and it bought a knighthood in the Invisible Empire of the Ku Klux Klan, where there were wizards, cyclopses, and kligrapps – and always someone else to blame. Although the Klan became an influence in state politics – it elected the governor of Georgia in 1922, a senator from Texas, and dominated the Oklahoma legislature – and for a time controlled Atlanta, Birmingham, Little Rock, and many smaller Southern cities and towns, it accomplished these feats of fleeting political power more by benefit of prejudice than of program. The Klan never had a platform and could never boast the powerful political leadership needed for long-term success. Most of the major urban newspapers of the day vociferously opposed it, and it ultimately fell victim to its own excesses.

Nevertheless, some of what it stood for, pinched and prejudiced as the Klan's expression of such things was, provided an insight into the mainstream of Southern culture. While not all white Southerners believed with the Klan that flogging and lynching were the best treatment for black Southerners who did not "know their place," virtually all white Southerners did agree with the aim of such excesses: the maintenance of white supremacy. Likewise, the Klan spoke endlessly of its determination to keep the South a Christian place, and there was never much doubt that it was anything else. Church membership in the South was higher than in other parts of the country, and three quarters of it was accounted for by Methodists and Baptists. The Southern Baptists grew by some thirty-five percent in the 1910s and 1920s, faster than any other denomination in America. Moreover, the influence of the churches far exceeded mere membership, and for many Southerners, urban as well as rural, the churches were the primary locus of social organization. They were also the primary institutional bastions of sectional distinctiveness, in an age when nationalizing tendencies in culture and the economy grew stronger every year. The Baptists, the Methodists, and the Presbyterians all remained divided into Northern and Southern branches, a rift that dated from the antebellum schism over slavery and that had still not healed eighty years later.

Southern churches were at this time as wedded to segregation as their predecessors had been to slavery, which partly accounted for the continued estrangement from their Northern brethren. But suspicion of the North also concerned matters of doctrine and the fierce opposition of orthodox Southern believers to what they perceived as heresy in the Northern church. The most notorious symbol of the controversy was the dispute between fundamentalist accounts of creation and Darwinian theories of evolution, which climaxed in the summer of 1925 with the trial of schoolteacher John T. Scopes in Dayton, Tennessee, on charges of violating the state's newly enacted prohibition on the teaching of evolution in the public schools. The trial was a thoroughly engineered affair: the American Civil Liberties Union wanted a test case and employed renowned Chicago lawyer Clarence Darrow for the defense; Dayton's civic boosters wanted to promote their town, which they certainly did when William Jennings Bryan – one of America's most eloquent orators and three-times unsuccessful candidate for the presidency – volunteered to prosecute. The trial occasioned some of the greatest legal theater in American history. Darrow humiliated Bryan on the witness stand, but lost the case anyway, before a judge who refused to admit scientific evidence. Scopes's conviction, however, was not the most important consequence of the trial. That was the new boost it gave nationally to the old image of the South as a backward and benighted place, immune to modern forms of enlightenment. The diatribes of Baltimore newspaperman H. L. Mencken on the alleged barbarities of Southern culture were the most famous among many such attacks for which the Scopes trial presented a large and irresistible target. If the Klan needed someone to blame, and predictably found that someone among Jews, Catholics, and blacks, so progressive opinion in the North rediscovered a mother lode of opportunities for easy criticism in the antics of the fundamentalist South. The result was not a pleasant spectacle, but it did illustrate the ambiguous response of Southerners toward change, and the still highly qualified nature of their relationship with the larger national culture. Chamber of commerce boosters touted the South as the ideal site for all manner of economic growth and development following the Northern model. And from Southern pulpits came dire warnings about the moral dangers of the modernism that was part of that same progress.

Right: *Teddy Roosevelt and his Rough Riders on San Juan Hill. In the Spanish-American War,* *United States troops came to the aid of Cuban rebels in their struggle to free themselves of Spanish rule.*

At the same time, a new kind of politician arose in the ranks of the Solid South. With the blacks effectively disfranchised, the struggle was between the old conservative Bourbons and the poor, white farmers and mill hands. The new Southern politicians, typically labeled "demagogues," preached their message against the iron-fisted control of the upper classes and played on the white rural class's fear of blacks. Among the more prominent demagogues of the early twentieth century were James K. Vardaman and Theodore G. Bilbo of Mississippi, Cole L. Blease of South Carolina, James E. Ferguson of Texas, and J. Thomas Heflin of Alabama. But perhaps the most famous and most able was Huey P. Long of Louisiana.

A native of Winn Parish, where antisecessionism, populism, and socialism held firm, Long entered public service as a member of the Louisiana Railroad Commission in 1918. As commissioner he solidified his reputation for looking after the interests of the little man by engaging the utilities in battle and winning reductions in the rates of telephones, electricity, gas, railroads, and streetcars. Although he was defeated in his first bid for the governorship in 1924 at the age of thirty, Long used that campaign to broaden his base of support, especially in the northern parishes. In 1928, when he again ran for governor, that support catapulted him to victory.

His first legislative program showed little divergence from the Progressivism sweeping through the South generally: a $30 million bond issue for roads and bridges; free textbooks and higher levels of funding for schools and charitable organizations. His roads program increased the miles of concrete roads from 296 to 2,446 and asphalt roads from 45 to 1,308, and the miles of gravel roads almost doubled by the end of 1935.

Despite the work of Long and other Progressive politicians, there was still some true substance in the image of the benighted South. There were lynchings, there were chain gains and forced labor, there was hookworm and pellagra, there was child labor, and there were inadequate schools. However, there were also Southerners in the liberal tradition who fought these things, with limited success. Newspapers such as the Charleston *News and Courier*, the *Norfolk Virginian-Pilot*, and the *Memphis Commercial Appeal* served as forums for denunciation of the more blatant Southern barbarisms. On the other hand, there were also Southern partisans in the conservative tradition – Donald Davidson, John Crowe Ranson, and Allen

Above: *born in Staunton, Virginia, Woodrow Wilson was elected president in 1912 and 1916.*

Below: *President Woodrow Wilson at his desk in the White House in 1919.*

Left: *coffins of the U.S. dead of the Spanish-American War await burial at Arlington National Cemetery. The cemetery stands on ground that once formed the estate of Confederate general Robert E. Lee.*

Tate, – who, while in no way defending lynching, put the case for the older Southern culture that allowed these things to exist because it also allowed other things to exist: religious piety and family life, a closeness to the land, a sense of history and psychological cohesion. Largely literary, they argued in images and metaphors and were no match in public debate for the voices calling wholesale for change. They found themselves on the outside looking in and sounded to many like hopeless Jeremiahs, yet the seriousness of their argument established them as social critics of lasting importance. In John Crowe Ransom's *God Without Thunder: An Unorthodox Defense of Orthodoxy* (1930), in Allen Tate's biographies of Stonewall Jackson and Jefferson Davis and in his poem *Ode to the Confederate Dead*, and in Donald Davidson's poem *The Tall Men*, there emerged a warning about the dangers of moral alienation that attended modernism and "progress." They published their agrarian manifesto, *I'll Take My Stand* in 1930, just as the latest New South, whose moral soundness they so doubted, collided head-on with the Great Depression. Their collaborators were Robert Penn Warren, Andrew Nelson Lytle, Stark Young, John Gould Fletcher, John Donald Wade, Frank L. Owsley, Lyle Lanier, H.C. Nixon, and Henry Blue Kline.

Above: *a gathering of the Ku Klux Klan in Homestead, Florida, and right, a 1926 Klan march in Washington, D.C. During the 1920s, the Klan experienced a revival and extended its repression to include foreigners, Catholics, and Jews as well as blacks.*

Throughout their combined work echoed the themes that tradition had fallen victim to modern industrialism and that the South was the only place left in America where the values of agrarian culture still had a chance to prevail over industrialized society. After the publication of *I'll Take My Stand*, the Agrarian writers found outlets for their philosophy in the pages of established quarterlies, the *American Review* in New York and the *Southern Review* in Louisiana. And six years after their first collaborative book, Allen Tate and Herbert Agar edited another collection, *Who Owns America?*, in which the authors protested against large corporate landowners and planters and rallied behind the yeoman farmers.

While the Agrarians were writing to persuade Southerners to take steps against modernity, another school of thought took shape in North Carolina. Regionalism, a synthesis of the social sciences, the humanities, and the natural sciences, had as its

leader Howard W. Odum, head of the School of Public Welfare and the Department of Sociology at the University of North Carolina at Chapel Hill. Odum began publishing the *Journal of Social Forces* in 1922 and founded the Institute for Research in Social Science two years later. His protegé, Rupert B. Vance, began publishing in the regional theme in 1929 with *Human Factors in Cotton Culture* and in 1932 *Human Geography of the South*. Instead of rejecting industrialism outright, Odum and Vance proposed that intellectual leaders at universities and enlightened industrialists could plan industrial development and agricultural reform in such a way that the traditional culture of the region would not be destroyed. In 1931, Odum received funding from the General Education Board for a regional study, and the resulting *Southern Regions of the United States*, published in 1936 became the final work of the regionalist school.

Regionalism pervaded not only the social sciences but literature as well. In 1929, Thomas Wolfe published *Look Homeward, Angel* and William Faulkner published *Sartoris* and *The Sound and the Fury*, the first of his novels focusing on Yoknapatawpha County. These books marked the beginning of the Southern Renascence, a literary period paralleled in American only by the New England Renaissance of the mid-nineteenth century. Among the many Southern writers were Erskine Caldwell, T.S. Stribling, Ellen Glasgow, Robert Penn Warren, Allen Tate, Andrew Lytle, Donald Davidson, Caroline Gordon, Stark Young, Katherine Anne Porter, Eudora Welty, and Carson McCullers.

In 1935 John Crowe Ransom advanced his theory on why Southern writers had suddenly sprung to such articulate life. The South had fallen victim to decay, according to Ransom, but rather than rush to espouse new ideals and new methods to effect recovery, the region's inhabitants and writers clung to the old ideals. The aftermath of the Old South's destruction in the Civil War brought out the most prolific self-appraisal. One of the first products of the new introspection appeared as *The Fugitive*, a literary magazine published between 1922 and 1925. In its pages were found the works of Ransom, Tate, Davidson, Warren, and others. Some of these writers, along with other students and faculty of Vanderbilt University, had taken to gathering for evenings of discussion at the home of Sidney Hirsh near the campus. After World War I, the gatherings moved to the home of James M. Frank, and their focus shifted almost exclusively to poetry. *The Fugitive* was born out of the accumulation of manuscripts brought by the writers to these meetings. Four members of The Fugitives – Ransom, Davidson, Tate, and Warren – went on to begin the Agrarian movement along with

Above: *William Jennings Bryan was the leader of Tennessee's prosecution team during the Scopes Trial in which John T. Scopes, a biology teacher in Dayton, Tennessee, was charged with teaching evolution, contrary to state law.*

other Southern writers. In addition, Ranson and Warren, along with Cleanth Brooks, became engaged in the "New Criticism," which espoused close readings of texts to determine meaning.

Apart from the Fugitive, Agrarian, and New Criticism movements, other Southern writers during the Renascence used their masterful eyes for detail and ears for dialect in countless novels whose actions takes place in the South. Thomas Wolfe, a native of Asheville, North Carolina, explored the themes of loneliness, isolation, and hatred and how they are overcome through sensuous experiences, love, and art in his four great novels, *Look Homeward, Angel, Of Time and the River, The Web and the Rock,* and *You Can't Go Home Again.*

Above: *William Jennings Bryan, a magnificent speaker in the cause of fundamentalism, speaking in Madison Square Garden in 1896.*

Left: *the protagonists in the 1925 Scopes Trial, left, Clarence Darrow, counsel for the defendant and the most famous lawyer in the nation, and right, William Jennings Bryan, prosecutor.*

Williams, Truman Capote, Peter Taylor, William Styron, Flannery O'Connor, and Walker Percy.

Prolific though the writers and theorists of the Agrarian and Regional schools were, however, it was not they but President Franklin Roosevelt who had the greater impact on Southerner's lives during the 1930s. Roosevelt, a New York blue blood with a house in Warm Springs, Georgia, always claimed to know the South well—indeed to love it and understand its problems. Southern politicians had been key to the new Democratic Party coalition of Northern labor and the Solid South that had put Roosevelt in office and kept him there for four terms, and under his presidential leadership Southerners enjoyed renewed prominence in the councils of the nation. Roosevelt was elected the first time on a largely conservative platform, and it was only when in office that he embraced a thoroughly pragmatic approach to dealing with the Depression.

It was Louisiana's Huey P. Long who posed the only serious threat to Roosevelt in the early 1930s. By then a senator, Long provided crucial help in securing the Democratic Party nomination for Roosevelt in 1932 and at first pledged support to the President. Two years after the election, that support evaporated as Long issued diatribes against the President's economic and labor policies. The President passed by Long in issuing patronage jobs in Louisiana, further angering the temperamental senator, who himself initiated a series of legislative measures designed to give him absolute control over the state.

Long's dreams were not bounded by state lines, however. In 1932, he announced his "Share-Our-Wealth" program, through which he proposed the liquidation of large personal fortunes, guarantees of $2,500 in annual wages to every worker, adequate pensions, and college educations for all qualified students. Two years later, he took his program nationwide and soon claimed that 7.5 million members belonged to his 27,000 "Share-Our-Wealth" clubs. His popularity soared to the point that poll-watchers estimated he could win six million votes as a third-party presidential candidate in the 1936 election. That prediction was never proved. In September 1935, Long was assassinated by Dr. Carl Austin Weiss in the Louisiana State Capitol. The presumed motive was that Weiss was infuriated over Long's attempts to oust Weiss's father-in-law from his judgeship. That too was never proved. After firing the shot that killed Long, Weiss was gunned down by the senator's bodyguards.

Unlike Long and his followers, most Southerners, as good Democrats and loyal party men, supported Roosevelt's New Deal legislation, and as long as it did not tamper with the region's racial arrangements nor threaten to disturb white supremacy even slightly,

William Faulkner wrote his huge volumes of works quite apart from any of the Renascence movements; in fact, he claimed to be a member only of "the human race." Themes of man's independence and individualism pervade his works, all but a few of which are set in Mississippi, specifically in the fictional county of Yoknapatawpha. A native of New Albany, Mississippi, Faulkner published his first book, *The Marble Faun* in 1924. Between 1929 and 1936, he reached the peak of his career, writing *The Sound and the Fury*, *As I Lay Dying*, *Sanctuary*, *Light in August*, and *Absalom, Absalom!*

Although Allen Tate proclaimed the Renascence over in 1935, more Southern writers would soon make their mark, among them James Agee, Tennessee

they proved themselves remarkably adept at trimming ancient prejudices about the dangers of centralized government power to the need for federal assistance in beating the bad times.

But even within many of the policies of the New Deal were embedded contradictions that proved daunting for Southerners, whose other heritage was fifty years experience with the promises and practices of the New South. The Agricultural Adjustment Act imposed crop controls in a region which had lived by its faith in an ever-expanding Cotton Kingdom for over a hundred years. In the non-agricultural sector, the National Industrial Recovery Act imposed codes of fair competitive practice and higher wages to put purchasing power back into the economy, in a region whose economic sages had long preached a low-wage policy as being key to the New South's industrial expansion. To fight against the campaign for higher wages, the Southern States Industrial Council was formed, and it argued that the South's traditionally low wages served the additional purpose of preventing pollution of the region's native labor pool by outsiders. The famous Section 7(a) of the National Industrial Recovery Act, which assured labor the right of collective bargaining, also grated on the laissez-faire, anti-union spirit of the New South.

As the source of less spiritual soul-searching, because its material benefits were more immediately apparent, the Tennessee Valley Authority (TVA) became one of the largest public works projects ever and represented the most massive ever federal program for the economic and social redevelopment of an entire region. That the region happened to be in the heart of the South made it all the more remarkable. TVA's genesis reached back to 1916 to the federal authorization, for reasons of national defense, of power and nitrate plants on the Tennessee River at Muscle Shoals in Alabama and to Nebraska Senator George W. Norris's belief that there should be a public yardstick for measuring the cost of private utilities. At stake was water power, the generation of electricity, the production of fertilizer, flood control, navigation, conservation, and other facets of regional planning; the project encompassed an area touching on parts of seven states and nearly as large as England. Whatever its government sponsorship, TVA became a powerful ally of the New South once recovery came, adding immensely to the region's attractiveness for industrial development. Ever since the 1880s, development-prone Southerners had boasted shamelessly of the abundance of the South's natural resources; only adequate capital for their exploitation was missing. The orchestration of resources by the TVA helped attract that capital anew, and the continued growth of textile and

garment manufacturing, paper milling and furniture manufacturing, and increasingly chemical and petroleum industries, seemed to prove that, despite the disadvantages of outside investment – and thus of outside control – if there were enough of it, then there would also be sufficient profits for the South.

Even so, the 1930s marked a period of economic stagnation for the South, as they did for the rest of the country. By the end of the decade, industrial production had returned roughly to where it had been in 1929. While economic growth during the entire period between the two world wars is impressive, and while the South's share of national economic production, as measured in workers and wages, actually rose, the fact of the South's relative poverty had not changed: its per capita income in 1940 was $340, compared with the national figure of

Above: *President Theodore Roosevelt was severely criticized by Southern politicians after he invited Booker T. Washington to dine at the White House. No gains for blacks, Southern or Northern, were achieved during Roosevelt's administration, however.*

Above: *Herbert Hoover won the Republican nomination for the presidency in 1928 and went on to win the election. After the stock market crash in 1929 and the subsequent economic depression, he was defeated in his bid for re-election by Franklin D. Roosevelt, who promised a "New Deal" for Americans.*

with the Supreme Court in a vain effort to remove that conservative obstruction to his economic reforms. The tactic frightened many people of a conservative constitutional bent, and it made many Southerners realize all over again the perils posed by an aggrandizing federal government. They also saw correctly that the whole course of Roosevelt's Democratic Party in the North, where its constituents were city dwellers, factory workers, and blacks, was in a direction decidedly unfavorable to the South.

Giving eloquent voice to that fear were distinguished Southern Senators – Harry Byrd and Carter Glass from Virginia, Walter George from Georgia, Cotton Ed Smith from South Carolina, and Millard Tydings from Maryland – who would henceforth oppose the New Deal. Their opposition so angered Roosevelt that in 1938 he tried to block the re-election of several of his Southern opponents – an episode remembered as the "Roosevelt Purge." He failed, and they were all returned to their seats, which was a repudiation of the president and a reminder that there were limits in the South that could not safely be passed even by someone as generally popular as Roosevelt. These limits sprang from the fundamentally conservative cast of mind of the Democratic New South leaders who still ruled the region. Like their predecessors in the 1880s, they dexterously courted the outside world for the material salvation it promised the Poor South – salvation that, in the 1930s, came in the form of federal spending as well as of Yankee investment. But, Southern to the core, they felt in their bones the potential dangers of such a courtship. It was a very old and persistent theme that the New Deal, in the context of the New South, highlighted once again: outside aid posed the threat of outside interference and ultimately of outside control.

This possibility was, of course, most frightening in the matter of race, and here two of the greatest themes of Southern history – racial adjustment and the fear of centralized government – began to converge once again. By the late 1930s, there were forebodings that the federal government might tamper with the racial status quo, just as it had recently tampered with the economic status quo, in the name of reform and a "higher law." The illusion of permanent superiority in matters of race, and all the myths of the New South that buttressed this, held secure for a few more years. But it took a willful blindness not to see, in the earnest efforts of Mrs. Roosevelt and her liberal New York friends on behalf of Southern blacks, in the impartial dispensing of federal relief to blacks as well as to whites, and in the restiveness of black Southerners themselves, that the South as white Southerners and their fathers had created it would not be the same for their children.

$575. If its losses during the Depression seemed less, it had had a far smaller distance to fall – and when it was all over and prosperity returned for good after World War II, the South still had the farthest distance to run just to catch up. The Depression had put the New South temporarily on hold, and the New Deal both sustained and subverted it. Canny Southerners, historically deft at getting what they wanted from the federal government while fending off unwanted intrusions, understood the value of liberal government spending policies for their poorly educated and capital-poor homeland. But as the Thirties wore on and as the New Deal swerved leftward in the direction of the welfare state during Roosevelt's second term, conservative Southerners, however addicted to the New South, sensed danger. In 1937, a frustrated Roosevelt attempted to tamper

7

STILL THE SOUTH?

The Second World War was shorter and less traumatic for the United States than for most of the other belligerent nations, but for a country that still clung tenaciously to old notions of innocence and isolation, it brought the cares – and the challenges – of the world crashing down on American shoulders with resounding finality. It was the first, and hopefully the last, great war of ideologies, and while it should have been the easiest war for the democracies to prevent, they found themselves sorely pressed, once it began, to meet and overcome the totalitarians' military might. That the democracies did in the end prevail was thanks largely to American involvement, which spelled not only victory for the Allies abroad, but change at home. Such a global conflict galvanized the country as nothing had done since the Civil War. The war was an unambiguous moral crusade to defeat a great evil, and once begun there was never any doubt about the necessity of carrying on to total victory.

But both the goal and the means employed to achieve it were loaded with important implications for the South, whose people once again eagerly flocked to their country's colors. Those implications meant change. The power of the federal government had grown enormously during the 1930s, and it was the attitudes and agencies of the New Deal experiment that were now pressed into wartime service and that lived on into the peace that followed to shape the evolving American welfare state. Even during the 1930s, Southerners had found themselves torn between old but still potent instincts about the virtues of small government and local and state autonomy on the one hand and the temptations of federal largesse on the other; the growth of federal power

Left: *at the 1948 Democratic National Convention in Philadelphia, picketers demanded equal rights for blacks and an anti-Jim Crow plank in the party platform. During Truman's first administration, he had founded a Committee on Civil Rights.*

that the wartime experience vastly accelerated set the alarm bells ringing in the South. World War II was also a fight against a particular manifestation of tyranny – Nazism – and was therefore a fight to the finish against a particular theory of the master race with all its attendant nightmares. The war was in part a moral battle against racism, and the implication of that battle for life back home in America – most notably in the American South – was not lost on blacks or whites for long. Moreover, the mere fact of the involvement of millions of military personnel with people from far-flung places – and of Southerners with other Americans in the ranks – had a bracing effect that dictated, when the troops finally did come home, some revision of old values.

The post-World War II era therefore witnessed the most sustained and deep-running assault on Southern sectional distinctiveness since the Civil War, and that assault is not over yet. This vast sweep of change is also the context for considering the history of the South in recent times. Is there, in the last decade of the twentieth century, a "South" worthy of the name left at all? And if so, what might its prospects be, based on the kinds of changes the region has both undergone and withstood in the years since World War II? The South unquestionably has a past, and a fairly distinctive one, whose themes persisted stubbornly into the 1930s. But in the light of recent historical experience, does the South have a future? Now, more than 130 years after the South made its supreme bid for independent status as a separate nation, is there still a "South" in the historical sense of the term, and what is its place in a united American nation?

To answer that question, it is necessary to view changes in key areas of Southern life in relation to the rest of the country. First of all, it is helpful to know the social and economic determinants that helped shape Southerners' lives and behavior. The framework for this is a familiar one and might well be described as the "New South Triumphant." The gospel of economic and social change that Henry Grady and his fellow travellers had crusaded for in the 1870s and 1880s seemed to take hold with a vengeance. But the difference now was that for the first time in the South's troubled pursuit of progress, the New South actually produced much of what it promised. The years after 1945 saw the development of the much vaunted "affluent society" in America, and Southerners made it known once and for all that they intended to be full partners in it. Traditionalist naysayers, those suspicious of the emptiness of materialism, were in short supply and decidedly out of fashion in these years. In their absence the booster spirit of the New South triumphed almost unconditionally. This pursuit of material prosperity

was not something that was done with much philosophical forethought, rather it was almost a reflex action. Rapid industrialization and the growth of cities were its most visible results.

In this latest rush toward the material good life, Southern boosters proclaimed afresh all the region's advantages: abundant natural resources and sources of energy, congenial state legislatures at the ready with favorable tax laws and other incentives, a cheap and plentiful labor supply, and long-deprived markets for durable and consumer goods. The conversion of wartime plants helped start the boom, which soon became self-sustaining as factories

Top: *segregated drinking fountains were standard throughout the South and were but one facet of the South's legal segregation system.*

Above: *in the 1950s, racial segregation was outlawed in intrastate transporation, as seen in this 1956 photograph from Norfolk, Virginia.*

Above: *despite the Supreme Court ruling on segregation on public transportation, in many areas passengers of different races continued to sit apart. Even after the Dallas Transit Company removed signs that instructed blacks to sit in the back of the bus, most blacks continued to move to the back for some time.*

Nordkarolina, Der Tar Heel Staat read the title of one pamphlet distributed to potential German investors. Southern states systematically profiled the attractions of their communities, from major cities to crossroad junctions, as sites for industrial development. Where old county governments were unequal to the challenge, local development districts were set up to promote industrial growth and to speed planning of the improvements in education, medical care, and public utilities that were needed to attract companies from outside the South. Southerners thus kept alive the old scalawag tradition of enticing Northern investment using the lures of relatively low expenses and high prospective profits. Large Northern-based corporations did enter the South to build plants and factories and hired Southern workers to man them. Management, while commonly non-Southern in the beginning, was eventually recruited from the native work force. Some of the new industry was not in fact all that new but followed the old pattern of resource extraction and the processing of agricultural products. Similarly, the old Southern prejudice against labor unions persisted and even became a major selling point with the promoters, who boasted of the South's supply of hard-working, nonunion laborers. In the 1940s and 1950s, ten Southern states enacted right-to-work laws aimed at the closed union shop, but such hostility was not limited only to the owners and managers. Many Southern workers betrayed their own aversion to unionization and, in so doing, showed themselves to be faithful scions of those contentious old Confederates who had resisted regimentation and limits on their individual freedom even during the desperate days of the Civil War.

Industrialization wrought very visible changes in the South's economic life. These ranged from the complete domination of the economies of small towns such as Camden, South Carolina, and Waynesboro, Virginia, by Northern-based corporate giants such as Du Pont and General Electric, to the complete remaking of regional landscapes. This is what happened in the Tennessee Valley where, by the early 1970s, the dams and power plants of the New-Deal-era Tennessee Valley Authority were turning out ten percent of the nation's electricity. Along the Mississippi River, oil refineries and petrochemical plants lined the shore all the way from Baton Rouge to New Orleans. Defense contracts provided an artificial, though highly tangible, boost to industrial growth, and as Cold War military budgets swelled, the South's share of them grew disproportionately. America's space race was run from Southern headquarters whose names became famous around the world in the 1960s and 1970s: Cape Canaveral in Florida, the Marshall Space Center in Alabama, and the mission control center in Houston, Texas.

multiplied, producing air conditioners, washing machines, farm implements and in time even automobiles, in addition to the old standbys such as textiles and chemicals. Exhibiting a zeal that matched the bonanza-sized opportunities, Southern leaders in both public and private life – governors, mayors, members of chambers of commerce and industrial development commissions – ceaselessly put the South's case as the undoubted site of America's next industrial revolution. North Carolina Governor Luther Hodges traveled some 67,000 miles in 1959 alone, promoting the advantages of his native state as a land of beckoning economic opportunity:

Change also came to the land itself, which remained for many Southerners, however they made their living, at the core of their identity. Once the "land of cotton" whose "kingdom" stretched from the Tidewater to Texas, the South of the post World War II years turned decisively to other more profitable commodities, and at long last it lived up to the New South's original admonition to farmers to diversify, diversify, diversify. By the 1960s, tree farms were as common as cotton fields and produced approximately a third of the nation's lumber; Southern pastures, which likewise profited from the region's generous growing season, fed beef cattle that produced an income for Southern farmers three times that earned by "the great white staple" of yore. Commercial poultry production soared, and from the long low-roofed sheds that became a fixture on thousands of Southern farms there came millions of chickens and turkeys and forty percent of the nation's eggs. More of a newcomer to Southern agriculture was the Asian soybean, a rich source of protein and fiber that was put to a thousand food and non-food uses and whose cultivation took the old cotton country of the Mississippi Delta by storm. Not that the old staple crops of the South's past suddenly disappeared, but their relative dollar value did decline markedly in relation to everything else. Almost all of America's tobacco continued to be grown in Virginia, Kentucky, and North Carolina, and the South still produced the lion's share of America's cotton, though most of it came from regions west of the Mississippi River. Louisiana, Texas, and Arkansas still cultivated some eighty percent of America's rice, and sugar occupied farmers in southern Louisiana just as it had in antebellum days. While "hog meat and hoecake" were no longer the monotonous staples of the average Southerner's diet, the South continued to produce pork and corn in great abundance, along with peanuts and sorghum and the fruits and vegetables that thrived in the region's warm, wet climate.

Such agricultural diversification and prosperity were not unique to the South in the post-1945 years, and in this respect, as in so much else, the South merely partook of larger national trends. The prosperity of the South's farms was accomplished using the labor of fewer and fewer Southern farmers. By 1970, only some 4.5 percent of the region's population, 2.3 million Southerners, still lived on farms, and the actual number of farms fell from 2.5 million in 1940 to under a million in 1970. There was however an irony for the South in this that did not afflict the nation as a whole. It was one of the prime myths, and realities, of agriculture outside the South that the small to mid-size owner-operated family farm was the optimum farming unit, for reasons as much cultural and moral as economic. Inside the

South, however, there had always been the countervailing myth, and reality, of the plantation, which from the earliest days of the republic had given Thomas Jefferson's image of the yeoman freeholder a tough run for its money. The rapid decline in the number of small farms after World War II ironically signalled a return to the old plantation farm. However, its modern incarnation usually came without benefit of white-pillared mansions and was obviously operated without either slaves or their post-Civil War sharecropper equivalents. The large commercial farms of this latest New South fitted squarely into established plantation tradition in scale alone. The new "plantations" were worked for profit by nonunion low-wage laborers operating all the mechanized cotton-pickers and corn-harvesters that the farmers could afford. "Corporate farming," as it has lately come to be derided in film and popular press, thus brought with it to the South historical associations that were missing in the rest of the country. This did not mean that there are still not thousands of New South salarymen who dream of retiring to that idyllic spread of rolling pasture or bottom land that their ancestors may well have abandoned for the milltowns of an earlier New South.

Whatever the ancestral pull of the land, the demographics of the post-1945 South told a different story. It was a story of the seemingly ineluctable migration of Southerners from the countryside and small towns to the cities. There had always been cities in the South, but most were places whose purpose was to service the needs of the surrounding countryside, or to serve as entrepôts linking the hinterland to the outside world. The sheer pace of urbanization in the twentieth century changed this, and at no time did the change happen faster than in the years after World War II. Industrialization speeded urbanization and breathed new life into old-fashioned towns such as Augusta, Georgia; Nashville, Tennessee; Montgomery, Alabama; and Richmond, Virginia. The South's premier city, Atlanta, Georgia, which had always made much of rising from the ashes left by William Tecumseh Sherman's Federal Army in 1864, set the pace, establishing itself as the commercial and transportation hub (first in the era of the railroad and later in the airline age) of the entire Southeast. Less than half a million people were living there in

Right: in 1957, President Dwight D. Eisenhower called out federal troops in Little Rock, Arkansas, to enforce the Supreme Court ruling, Brown v. the Board of Education of Topeka, *which struck down the "separate but equal" doctrine in place in American society since the turn of the century.*

Top: *in 1957, the only integrated school in South Carolina was St. Anne Parochial School in Rock Hill.*

Above: *in September 1957, Little Rock, Arkansas, opened Central High School to a few black students, but the governor*

called out the National Guard, whose members are shown here guarding the school, to bar the children's entry.

1940; thirty years later the figure was 1.2 million. Such growth was fueled publicly as well as privately. Thanks in large part to national defense spending, by the 1970s, the region as a whole received substantially more from the federal government in Washington than it paid in federal taxes. This, coupled with the enduring lure of a mild climate and a generally lower cost of living, gave birth to the Sun Belt phenomenon. The boundaries of the Sun Belt tended to vary from one newspaper report to another, and they frequently reached well beyond the bounds of the old Confederacy to states that were properly part of the West: New Mexico, Arizona, and California. But the old South was unquestionably at the core of the phenomenon and, to a nation whose Northern cities were increasingly wracked by crime, racial strife, and the decrepitude of greater age, the South came to represent a fresh start and America's

Above: *when six black students attempted to enter North Little Rock High School in September 1957, white students and adults repulsed them. Police officers finally escorted the black students away from the school.*

Above right: *white students taunt a black student attempting to enter Little Rock's Central High School in September 1957. Throughout the school year, troops remained at the school to enforce integration and protect the black students.*

newest land of promise – just as the old New South advocates had boasted.

Or so it seemed, as the suburbs of Southern cities sprawled in patterns of low-density development made possible by the pervasiveness of automobile transport and the paucity of public alternatives. Long after the wisdom of slicing through old urban districts with the "loops" of interstate highways had been questioned in the North, Southern cities were still calling for more roads as the keys to future progress. Southern cities grew out, not up, and they grew in a hurry. There was no time for, and little interest in, the agglomeration of dense inner-city neighborhoods; the Sun Belt cities sprouted in the middle-class, white-collar era, and because of an ethnic homogeneity utterly unlike the older industrial cities of the North, their residents tended to sort themselves along simple lines of income and, even

after *de jure* segregation was made unlawful, of race. In this sense, the cities' growth conformed to old Southern characteristics. But in their renewed promise of an utterly transformed physical and social landscape, the cities clashed sharply with the region's fundamental cultural conservatism. Atlanta boasted the first Hyatt House Hotel in America with a revolving rooftop restaurant, and, as in many other matters of urban style, this established a model that commercialized and homogenized Southern downtowns into a bland uniformity. It was as if the only alternative to the backwardness of the South's past lay with ever more modern and ever less critical versions of Atlantan Henry Grady's first New South of a century before.

That there would be costs of both a physical and cultural nature had been apparent from the beginning of that first New South, and the Southerners of the

Left: after the assassination of Martin Luther King, Jr., in Memphis, Tennessee, violence broke out in more than a hundred cities across the country. In Chicago, a man wears a placard announcing King's death as he watches looters in stores along the street.

post-World War II generations shared their fathers' ambivalent feelings about change even as they voted with their feet and their careers for progress. Along with industrialization came much environmental damage, of which even such a lauded agent of regional rejuvenation as the Tennessee Valley Authority could be found culpable, as a major consumer of strip-mined coal. Some areas, Florida in particular, seemed to grow too fast even for the most ardent promoters, and the cookie-cutter character of the sprawling subdivisions surrounding Southern cities distressed anyone who still nurtured an image of the South both as a place apart from the rest of America, and as a place that, because of its late development, should have been able to avoid some

of the mistakes made elsewhere. "Everywhere the past was going out with the times and the future coming on in a torrent," wrote Virginia novelist Ellen Glasgow back in 1922 about her native Richmond. "To add more and more numbers; to build higher and higher; to push harder and harder; and particularly to improve what had already been added or pushed – these impulses had united at last into a frenzied activity" is a description, and a lamentation, that is even more applicable seventy years later.

The single change in the South that very few actually lamented, and that no one would admit to lamenting anyway, involved the issue that most visibly went to the heart of Southern distinctiveness: race. The old "separate but equal" doctrine, which had governed race relations in the South in the 1890s, came under increasing pressure as a result of the fight against the Nazis in World War II, of the fall of the old colonial empires in Asia and Africa, and of a general shift in public opinion that said the overt nature of *de jure* segregation in public places offended fundamental American values. In 1954, the landmark Supreme Court decision of *Brown v. Board of Education* set aside "separate but equal" and opened the door on a tense period during which the forces of state and nation faced off as they had not done since the secession crisis of 1860 and 1861. This time no one talked of leaving the Union, but segregationist Southerners did make a series of creative last stands in a not altogether unsuccessful attempt to slow the steamroller of federally mandated racial equality. In 1957, Republican President Dwight D. Eisenhower sent federal troops to Little Rock, Arkansas, to protect black students at the newly integrated Central High School, and the next years witnessed much talk among Southern governors of "state interposition" and "massive resistance" to hold back the tide. They were not alone, and thousands of ordinary white Southerners rallied to their cry. But the times had changed decisively, and there were now thousands of native Northerners who had come to the South in the postwar economic boom and who were at best indifferent to the system of segregation. States' rights held little allure for them, and in the years of the "sit-in" and the "freedom march," the old racial arrangements of the South crumbled because of both outside pressures and internal weariness. Federal force was used again in the early 1960s against recalcitrant state governors such as Ross Barnett of Mississippi and George Wallace of Alabama, but it was the nonviolence of black leaders in the South, best exemplified by Martin Luther King, Jr., who had come to prominence during the Montgomery Bus Boycott of 1955, that eventually triumphed. The spectacle of peaceful black

demonstrators being met with the clubs and dogs and water cannon of white police departments, brought instantly into people's homes by television, revolted the moral conscience of the nation and moved moderate-minded people everywhere to the judgment that the South's racial prejudices no longer had a place in modern America. That consensus was reflected in the passage of the Civil Rights Act of 1964 and of the Voting Rights Act of 1965, which finally completed the work begun by the first Reconstruction following the Civil War. That the pattern of racial arrangements changed so quickly, and with so little social disruption, is testimony both to how truly outdated it had become and to the salient fact that white Southerners, who were in a majority in most parts of the region, no longer needed to fear the tyranny of a vengeful black majority.

The civil rights revolution, fought as it was by the plain people of the South, together with some from the North, occurred within a political context that itself reflected the changing realities of Southern life. Soon after World War II, the Solid South came under new strains as the Northern wing of the Democratic party – and the new president, Harry S. Truman from Missouri – forthrightly espoused the cause of civil rights. The presidential election of 1948 saw dissident Southern conservatives bolt from the Democratic Party to form the Dixiecrats, whose platform and candidate, J. Strom Thurmond of South Carolina, explicitly endorsed racial segregation. No Southern walkout occurred four years later, but disaffection with the liberal Democratic candidate Adlai Stevenson helped make possible the election of the first Republican to occupy the White House in twenty years, wartime hero Dwight D. Eisenhower. Despite the South's ancient habit of voting Democratic, the electoral votes of four border states – Virginia, Florida, Texas, and Tennessee – went to Eisenhower, who also cut deeply into the popular vote in every other Southern state except Mississippi and Alabama. The 1952 election also marked the beginning of significant "ticket-splitting" in the South, and of the resulting phenomenon of "Presidential Republicanism" even though the strength of the Democratic Party at the state and local levels remained for the time undiminished. Eisenhower also ran well in the South in 1956, though his second administration angered many Southerners over the troubles at Little Rock. In 1960, Southern fears deepened when the Democrats nominated, on the first ballot, the young liberal senator from Massachusetts, John F. Kennedy. Kennedy's running mate, Lyndon Baines Johnson from Texas, was chosen in classic ticket-balancing style to offset Kennedy's obvious weakness in the South. But it was Johnson, the master of back-room maneuver, who turned out to be the black man's

twentieth-century emancipator more than any Northern liberal. Ever the seeker after power, Johnson read clearly the writing on the wall, which said civil rights was the great cause of the decade, and skillfully made it his own. It was Johnson, the white Southerner, who guided the passage of the great civil rights bills of 1964 and 1965 through the Congress, and it was Johnson's signature that boldly made them law.

Through the 1960s, black voter registration rose dramatically, and the election of blacks to public office in the South became commonplace by the 1970s and 1980s. As the white South grew more enlightened on matters of race, or at least came to see the futility of overtly opposing change, its political behavior increasingly reflected other realities. Industrialization, urbanization, and suburbanization pushed the South's middle classes closer to the national mainstream than ever before. In the absence of the bogy of race, and despite the persistent populism that boiled to the surface in the third-party presidential bids of Alabama Governor George C. Wallace and, finally, in the election of Georgian Jimmy Carter to the presidency in 1976 on an anti-Washington platform, a sturdy Republicanism was developing among the prosperous citizens of this newest New South. By the 1970s, genuine two-party politics was being practiced all across the South, at all levels, for the first time since the 1840s, when the parties had been the Democrats and the Whigs. By 1980, the year that saw the ideological battle lines between right and left more clearly drawn than they had been in any presidential campaign, the conservative Republican candidate Ronald Reagan won the South solidly for the party of Abraham Lincoln, and repeated the performance four years later. Reagan's anti-statist message about the dangers posed to liberty by an oversized and intrusive federal government had great historical resonance in the South, though the reason for their concern was no longer the need to protect slavery or racial segregation, but rather the need to protect the still profound cultural conservatism of the region from the assaults of a rampantly egalitarian and secularist national culture.

It was not in politics but in religion – in the unadulterated orthodox faith of their fathers – that Southerners continued to find the solace of continuity amid rapid social and economic change. Even as ruralism and race have faded relatively as defining characteristics of Southern culture, the rock-hard militant Protestantism of the Southern Baptists, of the Methodists, of the Churches of Christ, and of the Southern branch of the Presbyterians qualifies as the greatest remaining conservator of Southernism. Sin to Southern Christians was a violation of divine law, not a consequence of a bad environment, and the

Left: *President Dwight D. Eisenhower.*

Below: *blacks stand in line to vote in Memphis. The Twenty-fourth Amendment outlawed state poll taxes in federal elections in 1964, thereby banning the traditional method used in Southern states to keep blacks away from the polls.*

problems of this world could best be addressed by a return to the moral precepts laid down in Holy Scripture. These churches offered a sentimental and transcendent brand of the faith that did not welcome social reform and did not encourage racial mixing even long after the battle for black Southerners' civil rights had been fought and won. Of all the institutions that could be said generally to serve the public, none have remained more impervious to racial integration than the churches, and not just the white ones. The black church, which provided so much of the nurturing ground and leadership for the great

victories of the civil rights movement, remains today almost totally black. On both sides of the color line, it seems, the church doors are wide open, but no one chooses to pass through of his own free will. Nor is it something that greatly troubles most Southern Christians, black or white. Both share deep Calvinistic doubts about the perfectibility of this world, and both have experienced over a long and tragic history together the futility of human efforts to bring salvation down to earth. In a world where, typically, much is desired and much more is promised, the skepticism about materialism that springs from Christian

orthodoxy may be the modern South's greatest remaining weapon in defense of a unique regional culture.

This book has been conceived as an illustrated history of the South, and the words and pictures in it will themselves, if they are at all worthy, come to stand as pieces of historical evidence – or simply as artifacts, if you will – of Southern culture in our time. There are pictures here of battlefields and plantations; of slave quarters and sharecroppers' shacks; of the high-born, the middling and the lowly, black and white; of Old South reactionaries and New South progressives; of bigoted segregationists and hopeful dreamers after racial brotherhood. There are also two images that do not quite fit any of these

categories but that help summarize, singly and together, the course of Southern history and perhaps portend something for the Southern future as well. Both come from the pages of *TIME* magazine, but twenty-eight years separate them. The first is an advertisement for the Southern Railway and above the copy, which begins "Two Hearts Beat As One," sit two heart-shaped pictures, one depicting an old Southern plantation house framed with live oak and Spanish moss and the other a modern factory festooned with well-used twin smokestacks and the American flag and fronted with a train belonging, naturally, to the Southern Railway. It dates from 1948, the year the Dixiecrats bolted from the Democratic Party. The second picture, which depicts

Above: *the Reverend Martin Luther King, Jr., leader of the Civil Rights movement.*

Above left: *a Greyhound bus burns in Anniston, Alabama, after a mob of angry whites attacked it.*

Left: *President Lyndon B. Johnson, who signed the Civil Rights Act into law in 1964.*

the Confederate stars and bars over a field of photographs of smiling little girls (black and white together), a white-columned mansion house, Atlanta skyscrapers, and a man kneeling in the attitude of prayer against a backdrop of the American flag, dates from 1976, the year of America's bicentennial and the year that saw a rural Georgian elected president of the United States.

They are images that speak in straightforward graphic language and are meant to communicate not just to the sensitive few but to the ordinary multitudes. What they communicate is the timeless war of the New South in all its forms against the tenacious older visions of Southern identity. That war has not been a simple one, and it has been fought

largely within the hearts and minds of Southerners themselves, where, quietly, it still rages. The images also illustrate the enduringly ambivalent relationship of the South with the rest of America. They are meant for non-Southern as well as Southern eyes and sensibilities; they are meant to flatter, to appease, to congratulate, to boast – and to persuade all who look upon them that the modern South and the modern nation truly are "one in all things essential to mutual progress and prosperity," but that they can still remain, to borrow the words of Booker T. Washington from a century ago, "as separate as the fingers of the hand" when it comes to matters of accent, cooking, manners, family, and faith. Nearly three decades apart, both images boldly assert, in the spirit of all the New Souths, that the region and the nation can have it all both ways: progress and tradition, change and continuity, material abundance and spiritual peace.

Yet both images also betray the doubt that so often subverts even the boldest professions of faith in creeds offering quick and cheap salvation from all history's woes. They reflect an abiding unease that has stretched across the most change-filled era in Southern history since the 1860s and 1870s. At the same time, they are an index of that change, for the pictures are not quite the same. While it may be hard to detect much change between the white columns of 1948 and those of 1976, it is plain to see that the purely "railway-industrial-smokestack version" of the New South in 1948 has become the "automobile-glass-towered-urban" New South of 1976. The people who appear in the 1976 image are old and new at once: the devout Protestant and the future flower of Southern womanhood, both black and white together – though it is the one little white girl who stands in the front and wears the eyelet and lace and the rhinestone tiara, while it is the three little black girls who keep to the rear, arrayed in plainer cloth and smiling wonderfully for the camera. These are curious and disturbing pictures, but useful ones when considering, finally, where the South now is in relation to its historical route.

Clearly, it is on the theme of race and racial adjustment that there has been the greatest observable change over the last century, and most of this has come during the lifetimes of Southerners still alive today. No one can fail to see and be impressed by the rapid and relatively complete undoing of the racial settlement that was reached back in the 1890s, which consigned black Southerners to separate and servile status. Behind that settlement had lain the old heritage of white supremacy that said, simply, that blacks were different and whites were better. The Jim Crow system of rigid racial segregation and discrimination that emerged in all its lurid detail in the first decade

of this century served white Southerners as slavery had served their antebellum forefathers. It was one of the axioms of their culture and the only thinkable means whereby two fundamentally different and hostile kinds of men could coexist with minimum strife and some modest degree of mutual benefit. That pattern of race relations – the rigid proscription of blacks and the assumption of superiority by whites – reigned largely unchallenged until well past the middle of this century and, wholly aside from what its moral and philosophical merits and demerits might have been, over the course of time it came to be a powerful habit with Southerners black and white alike, providing an ironic contrast with the nature of race relations in the region today.

Beginning in the 1940s and 1950s, the South's peculiar, and to many outsiders morally perverse, behavior on such matters, came under heavy fire from centers of opinion and power chiefly in the Northeast. By the early 1960s, it reached a crescendo unlike any since the 1860s, when another generation

of Northerners had tried so violently to reform and uplift the South. That first effort, though it had succeeded in its immediate goal of black freedom, failed completely in its longer-term implications of inviting blacks to share fully in the promise of American life. A century later, the tale would find a partly different ending because its tellers were different. The civil rights movement, sometimes called a second Reconstruction, would never have happened without the will and the power of the nation as a whole behind it: those were federal laws, federal marshalls, and federal troops that came crashing down on the once so secure South with all the awesome authority of assorted presidents, congresses, courts, indeed of the Constitution itself. The moral sense of the nation would no longer tolerate what it had been willing to tolerate sixty years before. Moreover, what the second Reconstruction had that the first one did not was a mobilized and increasingly articulate black population inside the South, willing to fight and bleed for its American birthright of

Above: *in attempts to end the Civil Rights movement, whites in Birmingham, Alabama, bombed the 16th Street Baptist Church in September 1963. Four black children were killed, and seventeen others were injured in the incident.*

Right: *Civil Rights workers enter a white waiting room and restaurant in a Montgomery, Alabama, bus depot in 1961. Montgomery was one of the most strictly segregated cities in the country.*

liberty. Without that, and the help of some courageous white Southerners, the nation would perhaps have found itself frustrated once again in trying to impose its reforming will on the recalcitrant South.

Thus Jim Crow came tumbling down and with him the hoary theme that the South was and must always remain a white man's country. Blacks drank from white water fountains, they went to white schools, they voted in what had once been lily-white elections, and they were themselves elected to positions of public power and responsibility. So, spurred by forces outside the region, black and white Southerners reached a new racial settlement to replace the old one. Or did they? The old racial settlement had been all-pervasive in nature; it had infused the public life and the private sensibilities of virtually all Southerners. The presumption of white supremacy governed, whether in the most public forum of politics or in the most private forum of domestic relations. This was not so with the new settlement. The latter, with which the South lives today, is largely a public matter. Even though outlooks have changed, the color line remains, more subtle than before but real nonetheless. For much of the

ordinary, everyday substance of people's lives is still beyond the reach of law and public ordinance. Where Southerners live, what churches they attend, whom they eat and drink with, whom they marry – these are still largely matters of personal choice, and there is very little to suggest that those ancient habits of racial separation that always made for one white South and one black South either have changed or will change. As the battle over public rights and entitlements receded into the past, its results acknowledged by all, whites came to realize that the sky would not fall if blacks voted and went to school with white children.

Much else certainly could be legislated for, and indeed had been in the South since World War II, which points to another old theme: the South's historically tortuous relationship with central government. Here, as in the matter of race, Southerners' performance has been a mixture of responding to new opportunities against a backdrop of old suspicions. The civil rights movement was the most obvious example of government intrusion in the region, but it was not the only one. The South, like the rest of the country, dutifully rose to the

Above left: *former president Jimmy Carter from Georgia sports a T-shirt promoting "Habitat," an organization that helps underprivileged people build their own homes and communities.*

Above: *President Jimmy Carter promoted a return to national pride after the fiasco of the Watergate break-in and cover-up during Richard Nixon's administration. He declared in his autobiography entitled* Why Not the Best? *"I am a Southerner and an American."*

tantalizing bait of the modern welfare state, which brandished its promises of vast, benign government assistance with this problem and that. Indeed, Southern lawmakers did much to bring the welfare state into existence. Its benefits and costs are something the South shares with the rest of the country. But the South's reaction to it has been different, for it has always been acted upon from the outside more than other regions – usually in the name of uplift, improvement, or justice, and frequently through the agency of government. The merits of what government and the welfare state are or aren't offering is not the point, except in a very general sense. Before the Civil War, the slaveholding South was faced with the old dilemma of liberty – the white South's liberty – or union. It opted for its own kind of liberty, with tragic results for all concerned. Today, in the wholly different circumstances of the middle-aged welfare state, that old dilemma might be transposed to read "liberty or security?" Southerners, remembering past difficulties with having it both ways, may yet choose clearly between the two. More likely they will hedge, like their fellow Americans, as long as they can. But when and if the time comes, those with any historical memory may have that uneasy feeling of having passed this way before. The anti-statist arguments that were narrowly applied by segregationist demagogues to fend off the steamroller of civil rights thirty years ago took on larger and more morally enlightened meanings as the entire nation moved sharply to the right in the 1980s, when the South more than any place in America could be called "Reagan country." How, and indeed if, this traditionally proud and conservative people can be reconciled to the welfare state at the end of the twentieth century is an open question, but wherever its ancient fear of central government may finally lead the South, there can be no mistaking the fear's powerful importance in the past.

The past has been even less yielding to assaults from within and without in another sector of Southern life; religious orthodoxy remains triumphant in the South. The South is still the most Protestant region of America, with three out of four church members calling themselves Southern Baptists, Methodists, or Presbyterians. Almost half of Southern church members are Southern Baptists, a denomination so all-embracing and so influential that it has fairly

Above left: *a "black is beautiful" parade draws a celebratory crowd. The concept was first promoted in the early twentieth century by W. E. B. DuBois, who said, "Beauty is black," and attempted to make blacks proud of their color.*

Above: *Governor George C. Wallace of Alabama attempted to win the presidential election of 1968 and campaigned for an end to the Civil Rights movement. In 1972, he campaigned against court-ordered busing and was showing strength in the primaries when he was shot by a would-be assassin.*

been called the folk church of the South. The secular impact of such religious identification, and of the faith it reflects, is notoriously hard to judge, but there can be no doubt that it contributes mightily to the conservative cultural cast of the region. It is often said that a people weaned on adversity cling to faith because they have known nothing else. If so, it is not surprising that Southerners, who until recently knew much about adversity, should have turned their gaze heavenward. On the other hand, this does nothing to explain the continuing growth of Southern churches throughout the balmy days of the present consumerist New South. It may simply be a truly indigenous – and a truly religious – phenomenon. Whichever, it continues to mark the South as being a place apart and to thrive profusely on the seemingly barren ground of modern secularist culture.

By contrast, another main theme of Southern history seems to have rather less of a future today, at least in the form that most Southerners once knew it. Ruralism is on the wane, and whatever parallels might be drawn between the small farms idealized by the Southern Agrarians who wrote *I'll Take My Stand* in the 1920s, and the "green revolution" of the

Above: *in the 1970s, the federal courts ordered busing to achieve racial balance in schools across the country.*

Right: *the South did not stand alone in its condemnation of busing. Here, a police escort leads a bus through Boston.*

1960s and 1970s, the fact remains that, by 1970, sixty-five percent of Southerners were classified by the census as urban. Yet this was urbanism Southern-style, and in most cases it was on a smaller scale than elsewhere. Only twenty-five percent lived in cities with populations over 100,000; forty percent lived in suburbs or in the 4,500 "cities" of less than 100,000 people. It is frequently remarked, with some justice, that most Southern cities, even the big ones, retain the quality of overgrown country towns. Indeed, many urban residents have only recently come from the country and still have ties there. And, in the 1970 census, there was that hefty thirty-five percent who were still officially "rural." These were not the rural folk of Jeffersonian myth: four out of five earned a living "in town," commuting by car to an office or factory, while remaining very much country people in outlook. And while the truly rural, agricultural

population was small, it remained divided much as it had been throughout its history into planters, yeomen, and landless laborers, with all the social distinctions to match.

Finally, poverty and a perceived powerlessness will cease to shape the South's future as they once shaped its past. The powerlessness of the South since the Civil War has probably always been overstated. For much of the last fifty years, certainly, the one-party Democratic South has managed to gain enormous influence in national councils, an influence far beyond what the region's numbers justify. Nor was the South powerless in all social matters: it regulated to perfection the most important of these – relations between blacks and whites. In addition, the romantic web so successfully spun around the old plantation culture created a myth of great social utility for the South's otherwise threadbare gentry – one that the Yankees were only too happy to be beguiled by. Poverty was another matter, however, and one that until almost yesterday was real enough for many Southerners. For the South was collectively saddled with its colonial economy, which sentenced it to never quite catching up. However, this is all now in the past tense. The new prosperity of the Sun Belt boom is not imaginary; this is the New South in the flesh at last, after all those years of blustery talk. And there is no reason to suppose that the new prosperity of the South will not grow even greater in the future. The region is still "behind," and it is no more recession-proof than the rest of the country. But the regional shift of power toward the Sun Belt is probably not a passing phenomenon. This means, ironically, that as the states of the old Confederacy become richer and more powerful, they will also become more American and less traditionally Southern. Their new wealth will be based on doing things that for years Northerners did before them, only Southerners will now be doing those things better, or at least more cheaply. But they will be using the script of a play that has been played before, and they will be speaking lines that once belonged to another. Henry Grady appears to have won at last.

Nor should it surprise that the region should at last have opted for Grady and his New South. Backwardness, after all, is picturesque only in fiction and old movies. Like Americans in colder climates, Southerners perceive the good life through a lens that is largely materialistic. They are subject to the same economic pressures and temptations as other people and, in general, they make their choices from the same broad set of options. And yet there remains a difference that is impossible to quantify and that has nothing at all to do with colonial economies, sharecropping, textile mills, or per capita income.

Left, right, and below: *photographs of children in North Carolina's schools from the early 1980s show the results of years of struggle by Civil Rights workers to achieve racial balance and harmony in Southern schools. The death toll for the concept of "separate but equal" was rung with court-ordered busing and voluntary integration of some communities.*

Rather, to use the Southern idiom, it is a matter of accent, and to talk about it is necessarily to deal with matters of taste and personal standards. Consider the following.

It is a cliché that any real Southerner will remain polite until he gets mad enough to kill. Not that many kill, though most are polite even in this age of "candor" and enlightened free expression. In sophisticated New South cities and on urbane university campuses, one can still witness a certain charming deference of man to woman, of youth to age, of student to teacher. Only the deaf can fail to notice the still pervasive "no, ma'ams" and "yes, sirs" that punctuate ordinary everyday conversation – leftovers for sure of a more class-conscious age but showing few signs of retreat even in these rigorously egalitarian times. Many of the rituals and restraints of etiquette that seem to have fallen out of use elsewhere still thrive in the South, perhaps less in their more outlandish Sir Walter Scott forms than simply as traditions of courtesy and good manners. Church, home, and family still serve as a prime source of social conventions and of cultural and moral values. Consciousness of kin – the saints and the sinners alike – remains powerful, and so, in a much attenuated form, does consciousness of class. Despite urbanization, industrialization, and the great movement of people and wealth into the South from the outside, a select gentry survives: descendants of antebellum planters who owe their continued existence more to the power of tradition than to money or influence, which have long since passed to others. There is a distinction in the South between "good family" and "good people" that is not often made in Iowa or Pennsylvania. Admittedly, it is only the shade of an aristocratic tradition, but one that, shorn of its less lovely trappings, has been redeemed. Its heirs can be stuffy and pretentious at their worst – undistinguished in either abilities or assets. But at their best, they can be a happy exception to the boredom and tastelessness of modern mass culture, where every man is automatically accorded equality with every other man and where all achieve a uniformity of low regard. By contrast, such character traits as personal integrity, honor, understated graciousness, and the cultivation of "good living" (as distinct from simply making a good living) are praiseworthy wherever they are found. "Who you are" may no longer, even in the South, take precedence over "what you do," but it does at least transcend "what you have."

Left: *Governor George C. Wallace of Alabama attends a reception in his honor in Washington, D.C. The governor was shot while campaigning for the 1972 Democratic presidential nomination.*

Return finally to the *TIME* magazine samples of the South's and the nation's image of this region. Though they are separated by twenty-eight years filled with momentous change, they share something that more than outweighs their differences. What they share is a delusion common to our times that concerns both our collective and our individual abilities and expectations. The Southern Railway advertisement from 1948 offers, in bold type and complete seriousness, the happy assertion that in Dixie "Two Hearts Beat As One." And the hearts are there for all to see – one overhung with factory smoke, the other with Spanish moss. The copy reads:

"The South has two hearts.

One is filled with the romantic charm and cherished tradition of bygone days ... yet it's still young and gay.

The other is the Southland's new, strong, industrial heart ... daring, courageous, optimistic ...beating with high hopes for the future."

So it is with the 1976 image. The confederate stars and bars cross over quadrants meant to proclaim the attainment of those things supposedly necessary to the good life in the modern South: religion, tradition, racial harmony, urban growth, and material success.

But is it believable that the ancient icons of the Confederacy can be made to embrace all the diverse components that this New South claims to consist of? The celebration of diversity has become the conventional wisdom of contemporary America, but is it not strange for the South also to be celebrating diversity? For, with good cause, generations of Southerners have celebrated not their diversity but rather their unity as a people. If they were diverse, it was a simple kind of diversity: some were black and some were white, and they lived on close and familiar terms and each knew just where the other stood. Nor is it really possible to believe that "two hearts can truly beat as one" – at least they can't for long. If they did in the now distant year of 1948, they certainly no longer do today. Both images rest on inflated expectations that the South, having finally emerged from its long historical travail, is truly charmed at last and is finally destined to have it both ways. Nineteen seventy-six proclaims all the happy harmony of modern pluralism. Nineteen forty-eight shouts more forthrightly: "Look Ahead – Look South!"

Of the two expressions of that shared delusion, the 1948 image is at least correct in suggesting, surely by accident, that in the end, in spite of, indeed increasingly because of, change, this matter of the South is truly a matter of the mind and heart. Those

two "hearts" in an innocent advertisement may be meant to convey outward harmony, but they also mask an inner strife, a fundamental war of the spirit that bedevils Southern history. It is a war, now as in the past, whose battles are fought, as those in most wars are, in indecisive engagements on relatively small, fields. For modern times in the South, it is a war in which the best tactics may be the careful trimming of expectations to abilities, while ever keeping in mind the question posed by the agrarian poet from Tennessee, Donald Davidson, of what it is we are, in comparison with what we are being asked to become.

Above: *the Captain John Smith Monument in Jamestown, Virginia. Smith's book,* A True Relation of Occurrences and Accidents in Virginia, *published in 1608, began a long tradition of writing about the region, attempting to understand the complexity and mystery of the South.*